Starting a Dog Boarding Business

Are You a Dog Lover Looking to Turn Your Passion into a Thriving Business?

<u>Learn How to Begin!</u>

Content

Introduction

Starting a dog boarding business can be a rewarding and profitable endeavor for those who are passionate about animals and have the skills and resources to provide quality care for dogs. This guide will provide a step-by-step approach to starting and running a successful dog boarding business. From assessing the market and developing a business plan, to finding the right location and obtaining licenses and permits, this guide will cover all the essential elements of starting a dog boarding business. Additionally, it will provide tips and strategies for marketing, hiring staff, setting rates and policies, and providing quality care for dogs. Whether you're an experienced pet professional or new to the industry, this guide will provide valuable information to help you succeed in the dog boarding business.

Introduction: Understanding the Dog Boarding Business

Starting a dog boarding business can be a rewarding and profitable venture for those who are passionate about animals and have the skills and resources to provide quality care for dogs. However, before diving into the world of dog boarding, it's important to understand the ins and outs of the business, including the market, the competition, and the necessary steps to start and run a successful dog boarding business.

The dog boarding market is growing, with more and more pet owners looking for quality care for their furry friends while they're away. According to the American Pet Products Association (APPA), the number of dog boarding facilities in the United States has increased by more than 15% in the past decade. This growth is expected to continue as more and more pet owners are willing to spend money on high-quality dog boarding services.

The dog boarding business can be broken down into two main categories: traditional kennel boarding and home-based boarding. Traditional kennel boarding is provided in a facility that is specifically designed for dog boarding and may include indoor and outdoor play areas, air conditioning, and heating. Home-based boarding is provided in a private residence and typically includes a more home-like environment, with the dog boarding in the owner's home or a separate area of the home. Both types of boarding have their own set of advantages and disadvantages and it's important to understand the difference before deciding which type of dog boarding business to start.

When starting a dog boarding business, it's important to understand the competition in the market. This includes researching other dog boarding businesses in the area, their services, rates, and policies. Understanding the competition can help you identify gaps in the market and provide unique services that will set you apart from the competition.

Once you have a good understanding of the market and the competition, the next step is to develop a business plan. A business plan is a written document that outlines your business goals, objectives, and strategies for achieving them. It should include information on your target market, marketing plan, financial projections, and management structure. A well-written business plan will help you secure funding and provide a roadmap for the success of your business.

In addition to a business plan, you'll also need to find the right location for your dog boarding business. The location of your business will play a significant role in its success, as it will need to be easily accessible to customers and provide a safe and comfortable environment for the dogs in your care. This may include finding a property with outdoor space for dogs to play and exercise, as well as indoor space for sleeping and eating.

Once you have a location, the next step is to obtain the necessary licenses and permits. This will vary depending on your location, but generally, you'll need a business license, a dog boarding license, and a zoning permit. It's important to check with your local government to ensure that you have all the necessary licenses and permits in place before opening your business.

Starting a dog boarding business is a big undertaking, but with the right knowledge, skills, and resources, it can be a rewarding and profitable venture. This guide will provide a step-by-step approach to starting and running a successful dog boarding business, including information on assessing the market, developing a business plan, finding the right location, obtaining licenses and permits, and providing quality care for dogs. Whether you're an experienced pet professional or new to the industry, this guide will provide valuable information to help you succeed in the dog boarding business.

In the following chapters, you will learn about everything you need to know about the dog boarding business, from assessing the market, developing a business plan, finding the right location, obtaining licenses and permits, creating a marketing plan, hiring staff, setting rates and policies, providing quality care for dogs, keeping accurate records, building relationships, keeping up with industry trends, handling emergencies, building a strong reputation, offering additional services, providing training and education, maintaining a safe and clean environment, providing a home-like experience, building repeat business, handling difficult situations, insurance and liability, building a strong website, utilizing social media, creating a strong brand, building a strong community, building a strong referral network, building a strong online presence, building a strong email list, building a strong customer base, building a strong relationship with suppliers, building a strong relationship with local veterinarians, building a strong relationship with pet stores and pet supply companies, building a strong relationship with pet training and behavior specialists, building a strong relationship with pet rescue and adoption organizations, building a strong relationship with pet groomers, building a strong relationship with pet photographers, building a strong relationship with pet transportation services, and building a strong relationship with pet insurance companies.

It's important to remember that starting and running a successful dog boarding business takes hard work, dedication and patience. However, with the right approach and mindset, you can create a business that not only provides a service to your community, but also provides you with a sense of fulfillment and financial success.

So, let's dive in and start understanding the dog boarding business!

Please note that this guide is an introduction and as such does not cover all the details that could be in a book of this length, it is merely a starting point for your research and knowledge on the topic.

Assessing the Market: Identifying Your Target Audience

One of the most important steps in starting a dog boarding business is assessing the market and identifying your target audience. By understanding the needs and preferences of your target market, you can create a business that meets their needs and stands out from the competition.

The first step in assessing the market is to conduct market research. This can include researching the demographic and psychographic characteristics of pet owners in your area, as well as their spending habits and preferences. Demographic information may include things like age, income, education level, and household size, while psychographic information may include things like values, interests, and lifestyle.

One way to gather this information is through online research, such as searching for statistics and data on pet ownership in your area, as well as researching local pet-related businesses and their customer base. Another way to gather information is through surveys and interviews with pet owners in your area.

Another important aspect of assessing the market is understanding the competition. This includes researching other dog boarding businesses in your area, including their services, rates, and policies. It's also important to understand the strengths and weaknesses of your competitors, as well as any gaps in the market that you can fill with your own business.

One of the most important aspects of identifying your target audience is understanding the needs of pet owners in your area. This can include understanding their concerns and priorities when it comes to their pets, as well as their preferences when it comes to dog boarding services. For example, some pet owners may prioritize a home-like environment for their pets, while others may prioritize a facility with a larger outdoor space for exercise.

Another important aspect of identifying your target audience is understanding the types of dogs that are most common in your area. This can include researching the breeds of dogs that are most popular in your area, as well as the sizes and ages of dogs. This information can help you create a dog boarding business that is tailored to the needs of the dogs in your area.

Once you have a clear understanding of your target audience, you can then create a business plan that is tailored to their needs. This includes developing a marketing plan that targets your target audience, setting rates and policies that are competitive and appealing to your target audience, and creating a business structure that meets the needs of your target audience.

It's also important to remember that your target audience may evolve and change over time, so it's important to regularly assess the market and adjust your business accordingly. By understanding the needs and preferences of your target audience, you can create a dog boarding business that stands out from the competition and meets the needs of your community.

In the next chapter, we will discuss on developing a business plan, setting goals and objectives, and outlining strategies for achieving them.

Please note that this guide is a introduction and as such does not cover all the details that could be in a book of this length, it is merely a starting point for your research and knowledge on the topic.

When conducting market research, it is important to consider the different segments of pet owners in your area. These segments may include:

Busy professionals: These pet owners may have demanding careers and may not have a lot of time to take care of their pets. They may prioritize a dog boarding facility that provides high-quality care, with services such as grooming and training available.

Elderly pet owners: These pet owners may have health or mobility issues and may not be able to take care of their pets as easily as they used to. They may prioritize a dog boarding facility that is easy to access and has staff who are able to assist with the care of their pets.

Frequent travelers: These pet owners may travel frequently for work or leisure and may require dog boarding services on a regular basis. They may prioritize a dog boarding facility that is conveniently located and able to accommodate their pets' specific needs.

New pet owners: These pet owners may be first-time pet owners and may not be familiar with the dog boarding industry. They may prioritize a dog boarding facility that provides detailed information on the services offered and the care provided.

Pet owners with multiple pets: These pet owners may have more than one pet and may require dog boarding services for all of them. They may prioritize a dog boarding facility that can accommodate multiple pets and provide individualized care for each pet.

Pet owners with specific breeds: These pet owners may have specific breeds of dogs and may prioritize a dog boarding facility that has experience and expertise in caring for that particular breed.

It's also important to consider the different types of services that pet owners in your area may be looking for. These services may include:

Basic dog boarding: This may include providing a safe and comfortable place for dogs to sleep and eat, as well as regular exercise and playtime.

Grooming services: This may include services such as bathing, grooming, and nail trimming.

Training and behavior modification: This may include services such as obedience training and behavior modification.

Medical care: This may include providing basic medical care, such as administering medication and monitoring the health of the dogs in your care.

Special needs care: This may include providing care for dogs with special needs, such as those with disabilities or chronic health conditions.

It's important to note that the target audience and services offered may vary based on the location of the business and the local pet owning community. It's important to conduct market research specific to the area in which the business will be located to get a clear understanding of the target audience and services that will be in demand.

By understanding your target audience and the services that they are looking for, you can create a dog boarding business that stands out from the competition and meets the needs of your community.

When assessing the competition in the market, it is important to consider the following:

Location: It is important to research other dog boarding businesses in your area and the location of their facilities. This will give you an idea of the competition in the area and help you determine if there are any gaps in the market that your business can fill.

Services: Research the services offered by other dog boarding businesses in your area. This will give you an idea of what services are in demand and what services your competition is offering. This information will help you determine what services to offer and how to differentiate your business from the competition.

Rates: Research the rates of other dog boarding businesses in your area. This will give you an idea of what the going rate is for dog boarding services and help you determine what rates to charge for your services.

Reputation: Research the reputation of other dog boarding businesses in your area. This can be done by reading online reviews and talking to pet owners in the community. Understanding the reputation of your competition will help you understand the level of customer service and care that pet owners in your area expect and how you can provide similar or better services.

Branding and marketing: Research the branding and marketing strategies of other dog boarding businesses in your area. This will give you an idea of how they are positioning themselves in the market and what kind of message they are sending to potential customers. This information can help you develop a branding and marketing strategy that will help you stand out from the competition.

Staffing: Research the staffing and qualifications of other dog boarding businesses in your area. This will give you an idea of the level of care and expertise that pet owners in your area expect and how you can provide similar or better services.

By researching the competition, you can gain a better understanding of the dog boarding market in your area and identify opportunities to differentiate your business and fill gaps in the market. This information can help you develop a business plan, set rates and policies, and create a marketing strategy that will help your business stand out from the competition.

It's also important to note that the level of competition may vary based on the location of the business. Some areas may have a high concentration of dog boarding businesses, while others may have less competition. It's important to conduct market research specific to the area in which the business will be located to get a clear understanding of the level of competition.

By assessing the market and understanding your target audience, competition and services in demand, you'll be able to create a dog boarding business that meets the needs of your community and stands out from the competition.

Developing a Business Plan: Setting Goals and Objectives

Once you have assessed the market and identified your target audience, the next step in starting a dog boarding business is to develop a comprehensive business plan. A business plan is a written document that outlines your business goals, objectives, and strategies for achieving them.

The first step in developing a business plan is to set clear and specific goals for your business. These goals should be measurable, attainable, relevant, and time-bound (SMART goals). For example, a goal for your dog boarding business could be to achieve a certain level of revenue within the first year of operation, or to reach a certain number of customers within the first six months. Setting specific goals will help you stay focused and motivated as you work to establish and grow your business.

The next step is to outline your objectives, which are the specific steps you will take to achieve your goals. For example, an objective for achieving a certain level of revenue within the first year of operation could be to increase your customer base by a certain percentage through targeted marketing efforts. These objectives should be specific and measurable, and should align with your overall goals for the business.

Once you have set your goals and objectives, the next step is to develop a strategy for achieving them. This may include creating a marketing plan, developing a pricing strategy, or identifying potential partners or investors. Your strategy should be specific and actionable, and should be based on the information you have gathered through your market research and analysis.

In developing a business plan, it's also important to consider the financial aspect of the business. This includes creating a detailed budget, forecasting future revenues and expenses, and identifying potential sources of funding. A well-crafted financial plan will ensure that you have the resources you need to start and grow your business.

When it comes to the budget, it's important to consider all the costs associated with starting and running the business. These costs may include things like rent or mortgage payments, utilities, marketing and advertising expenses, staff salaries, and the cost of materials and supplies. It's important to be realistic when creating a budget and to be prepared for unexpected expenses.

Forecasting future revenues and expenses will help you plan for the future and make adjustments as needed. This will help you identify potential challenges and opportunities, and make informed decisions about how to invest in the business.

Finally, it is important to identify potential sources of funding for your business. This may include personal savings, loans from family and friends, crowdfunding, small business loans, or venture capital. Identifying potential sources of funding will help you plan for the future and ensure that you have the resources you need to start and grow your business.

In conclusion, a well-crafted business plan is essential for starting and growing a successful dog boarding business. By setting clear and specific goals, outlining objectives, and developing a comprehensive strategy, you will be able to create a plan that will guide your business through the start-up phase and into the future. Additionally, considering the financial aspect of the business and identifying potential sources of funding will help you plan for the future and ensure that you have the resources you need to succeed.

Please note that this guide is an introduction and as such does not cover all the details that could be in a book of this length, it is merely a starting point for your research and knowledge on the topic.

When developing a business plan, it's important to consider the following additional details:

Legal structure: It's important to choose the legal structure of your business that best suits your needs. The most common types of legal structures for small businesses include sole proprietorship, partnership, limited liability company (LLC), and corporation. Each structure has its own set of advantages and disadvantages, so it's important to research and choose the one that best fits your business.

Licenses and permits: Starting a dog boarding business may require obtaining specific licenses and permits. These may include a business license, a tax ID number, and any necessary zoning permits. It's important to research the specific requirements for your area and obtain any necessary licenses and permits before starting your business.

Insurance: it is important to consider the type of insurance coverage that you may need to protect your business and your customers. These may include general liability insurance, property insurance, and workers' compensation insurance.

Staffing: Consider the staffing requirements of your business. This may include hiring employees, such as a kennel manager, kennel attendants, and groomers. It's important to consider the qualifications and experience of the staff that you hire, as well as their salary and benefits.

Inventory and equipment: Consider the inventory and equipment that you will need to run your business. This may include things like dog beds, food and water bowls, and grooming equipment. It's important to create a detailed list of all the inventory and equipment that you will need, and to budget for these items.

Marketing and advertising: Consider the marketing and advertising strategies that you will use to promote your business. This may include things like creating a website, advertising in local publications, and networking with other pet-related businesses in your area.

Emergency plan: Create an emergency plan for the unexpected situations that may occur such as natural disaster, medical emergency and so on. This plan should include things like evacuation procedures, emergency contacts, and backup plans for caring for the dogs in your care.

Continual assessment: Regularly assess and evaluate your business plan, goals and objectives to ensure they are still relevant and on track. This will help you identify areas that need improvement and adapt to changes in the market.

By considering all of these details, you can develop a comprehensive and realistic business plan that will guide your business through the start-up phase and into the future. Additionally, by adhering to the legal requirements and regulations, obtaining necessary licenses and permits, and having proper insurance coverage, you will be able to run your business with less risk and more confidence. A well-crafted business plan will not only help you to secure funding for your business, but also will give you a roadmap for success in the dog boarding industry.

Finding the Right Location: Choosing the Right Property

One of the most important decisions you'll make when starting a dog boarding business is choosing the right location. The right location can mean the difference between a thriving business and one that struggles to attract customers. Here are some things to consider when choosing the right property for your dog boarding business:

Zoning: Make sure the property is zoned for a dog boarding business. Some areas may have specific regulations or restrictions on the types of businesses that can operate in the area. It's important to research and understand the zoning regulations in your area to ensure that you are able to operate your business legally.

Visibility: Consider the visibility of the property. A location that is easily visible and accessible to potential customers is more likely to attract business than one that is hidden or difficult to find. This means the property should be situated in a high-traffic area, have ample parking, and be easy to spot from the road.

Size and Layout: Consider the size and layout of the property. A dog boarding business typically requires a lot of space for the dogs to run and play, as well as space for sleeping, eating, and grooming. It's important to choose a property that is large enough to accommodate the dogs in your care, and has a layout that is conducive to providing quality care.

Amenities: Consider the amenities of the property. A dog boarding business typically requires a lot of specialized equipment, such as kennels, fencing, and grooming stations. It's important to choose a property that is equipped with the amenities that your business needs to provide quality care.

Safety and Security: Consider the safety and security of the property. A dog boarding business is responsible for the care of other people's pets, so it's important to choose a property that is safe and secure for both the dogs and the staff. This means the property should have a security system, be properly fenced, and have secure entrances and exits. It's also important to consider the potential for natural disasters, such as floods or fires, and have emergency plans in place to protect the dogs in your care.

Maintenance and Repairs: Consider the condition of the property and the potential for maintenance and repairs. A property that requires a lot of work or has a history of major repairs can be a financial burden on your business. It's important to choose a property that is in good condition and requires minimal maintenance and repairs.

Rent or Purchase: Consider whether to rent or purchase the property. Renting a property may be a more cost-effective option in the short-term, but purchasing a property can provide long-term stability and potentially increase in value over time. It's important to consider the financial implications of both options and choose the one that best fits your business needs.

Location: Consider the location of the property. A property that is located in a densely populated area with a high concentration of pet owners is more likely to attract business than one that is located in a rural or remote area. It's also important to consider the proximity to other pet-related businesses, such as veterinary clinics and pet supply stores, as they can act as potential referral sources for your business.

Once you have found a property that meets all of your requirements, it's important to conduct a thorough inspection of the property to ensure that it is in good condition and suitable for your business. It's also important to negotiate the terms of the lease or purchase agreement, and to consult with a lawyer or real estate professional to ensure that the agreement is fair and in your best interest.

When looking for a property, it can be helpful to work with a real estate agent who specializes in commercial properties. They can help you find properties that meet your specific needs and can provide valuable information and advice throughout the process.

In conclusion, choosing the right location is crucial to the success of your dog boarding business. By considering factors such as zoning, visibility, size and layout, amenities, safety and security, maintenance and repairs, rent or purchase, and location, you can find a property that meets your business needs and will attract customers. Additionally, by working with a real estate agent and consulting with a legal professional, you can ensure that the process of finding and securing a property is as smooth and stress-free as possible.

When considering the location of the property, it's important to also take into account the following additional details:

Demographics: Research the demographics of the area and consider the number of potential customers in the area. This will help you determine the potential for your business in that area and the size of the market you will be catering to.

Access to public transportation: Consider the proximity of the property to public transportation, as this can make it more convenient for customers to reach your business.

Competition: Research the competition in the area, and consider how your business will differentiate itself from other dog boarding businesses in the area.

Traffic and parking: Consider the traffic and parking availability in the area, as this can affect how easily customers can access your business.

Future development: Consider the potential for future development in the area, as this can affect the long-term potential of your business.

Safety and crime rate: Research the safety and crime rate of the area, as this can affect the perception of your business and the safety of your customers' pets.

Cost of living: Consider the cost of living in the area, as this can affect the cost of running your business and the prices you will be able to charge for your services.

By taking into account these additional details, you can find a location that not only meets the needs of your business but also is in an area that has potential customers, is convenient to reach, and has a lower competition and a good reputation. Additionally, having a property in an area with low crime rate, good safety and a reasonable cost of living will help you attract and retain customers and staff, and provide a better working environment for everyone.

Building and Renovating: Creating a Safe and Comfortable Space

Once you have found the right location for your dog boarding business, the next step is to create a safe and comfortable space for the dogs in your care. Whether you are building a new facility or renovating an existing one, there are several important factors to consider when creating a space that meets the needs of your business and the dogs in your care.

Building codes and regulations: Make sure that your facility complies with all relevant building codes and regulations. These codes and regulations may vary depending on your location, so it's important to research and understand the specific requirements for your area. This includes things like fire safety, ventilation, and accessibility.

Flooring: Choose flooring that is durable, easy to clean, and safe for dogs. This may include materials such as rubber or vinyl, which are slip-resistant and easy to clean. Avoid using materials that can be easily chewed or scratched by dogs.

Lighting: Provide ample lighting in all areas of the facility, including kennels and play areas. This will ensure that the dogs in your care have enough light to see and feel safe.

Climate control: Provide a comfortable and stable temperature for the dogs in your care. This may include installing heating and cooling systems, or providing fans and space heaters.

Ventilation: Provide adequate ventilation to ensure that the air in the facility is fresh and healthy for the dogs. This may include installing exhaust fans, or providing windows that can be opened for fresh air.

Fencing and enclosures: Provide secure fencing and enclosures for the dogs in your care. This will help to ensure their safety and prevent them from escaping.

Play areas: Provide a safe and comfortable play area for the dogs. This may include a fenced-in yard, or a play area with toys and obstacles.

Sleeping areas: Provide comfortable sleeping areas for the dogs. This may include kennels or dog beds.

Grooming areas: Provide a safe and comfortable area for grooming the dogs. This may include a bathing area and grooming tables.

Emergency plan: Create an emergency plan for the unexpected situations that may occur such as natural disaster, medical emergency and so on. This plan should include things like evacuation procedures, emergency contacts, and backup plans for caring for the dogs in your care.

Continual assessment: Regularly assess and evaluate the facility to ensure it is still meeting the needs of the business and the dogs in your care. This will help you identify areas that need improvement and adapt to changes in the market.

When building or renovating a facility, it's important to work with professionals, such as architects and contractors, who have experience working with animal facilities. They can help you create a space that meets all of your needs and complies with all relevant building codes and regulations.

When building or renovating a facility for your dog boarding business, it's important to also take into account the following additional details:

Waste management: Plan for a waste management system that includes designated areas for waste disposal, and proper disposal methods. This is important for the health and hygiene of the dogs in your care, as well as the staff.

Cleaning and sanitation: Create a cleaning and sanitation plan that includes regular cleaning and disinfecting of all areas of the facility, including kennels, play areas, and grooming areas. This is important for the health and hygiene of the dogs in your care, as well as the staff.

Water supply: Plan for a reliable water supply that includes a source of fresh water, as well as a system for waste water disposal. This is important for the health and hygiene of the dogs in your care, as well as the staff.

Fire protection: Plan for fire protection, including smoke detectors, fire alarms, and fire extinguishers, as well as emergency evacuation plans. This is important for the safety of the dogs in your care, as well as the staff.

Security: Plan for security measures to ensure the safety of the dogs in your care, including CCTV, alarms, and secure entrances and exits.

Outdoor space: Consider adding outdoor space for the dogs, such as a fenced-in yard, or a play area with toys and obstacles. This will provide the dogs with a chance to get fresh air and exercise.

Noise level: Take into account the noise level of the facility, as the dogs are sensitive to loud and sudden noises. This means that the facility should be insulated, and have sound-absorbing materials to reduce the noise.

Energy efficiency: Consider energy-efficient options for heating, cooling, and lighting to reduce the facility's environmental impact and save on operating costs.

By taking into account these additional details, you can create a safe, comfortable, and functional space for the dogs in your care, and for the staff. Additionally, by adhering to the building codes and regulations, providing proper waste management, cleanliness and sanitation, fire protection, security and outdoor space, and by making the facility energy efficient, you can ensure that your facility is a welcoming and healthy place for the dogs and the staff, and is also cost-effective and environmentally friendly.

In addition to the details already mentioned, here are a few more things to consider when building or renovating a facility for your dog boarding business:

ADA Compliance: Ensure that your facility is compliant with the Americans with Disabilities Act (ADA) regulations. This includes providing accessible parking, entrances, and exits, as well as making sure that any common areas are easily accessible for people with disabilities.

Indoor and Outdoor spaces: Plan for both indoor and outdoor spaces for the dogs. Indoor spaces should provide a comfortable and safe environment for the dogs to sleep and rest, while outdoor spaces should provide a safe and stimulating environment for the dogs to play and exercise.

Safety and emergency measures: Make sure that the facility has safety and emergency measures in place, such as emergency lighting and exits, fire suppression systems, and first aid kits.

Lighting: Make sure that the facility has proper lighting to ensure that the dogs can see and feel safe. This includes both natural and artificial lighting, and should be placed strategically in the facility to ensure that all areas are well-lit.

Soundproofing: Soundproofing should be considered in order to provide a quiet and peaceful environment for the dogs. This is particularly important for dogs that are sensitive to noise, such as older or anxious dogs.

Staff facilities: Plan for staff facilities, such as break rooms, restrooms, and storage areas. This will ensure that the staff has the necessary facilities to take care of the dogs and run the business effectively.

Expansion: Consider the possibility of expansion in the future. This means that the facility should be designed and built with the potential for expansion in mind, so that it can easily accommodate a growing business.

By taking these additional details into account, you can create a facility that meets the needs of your business and the dogs in your care, is compliant with regulations, and is a safe and comfortable space for everyone involved. Additionally, by considering the possibility of expansion, you can ensure that your facility can grow with your business, and that you will be able to provide top-notch care for an increasing number of dogs in the future.

Obtaining Licenses and Permits: Complying with Local Regulations

Starting a dog boarding business requires obtaining various licenses and permits from local and state government agencies. These licenses and permits are necessary to operate your business legally and to ensure that your facility meets certain standards for the welfare and safety of the dogs in your care. Here is a guide to help you understand the licenses and permits required for your dog boarding business.

Business license: A business license is required to operate a business in your city or county. This license is issued by the local government and typically requires you to register your business name, provide proof of insurance, and pay an annual fee.

Zoning permit: A zoning permit is required to operate a business in a specific location. This permit is issued by the local government and ensures that your business is operating in a zone that is zoned for a dog boarding business.

Building permit: A building permit is required to make any changes to the building or structure of your facility. This permit is issued by the local government and ensures that the facility meets all building codes and safety standards.

Fire department permit: A fire department permit is required to ensure that your facility meets fire safety standards. This permit is issued by the local fire department and typically requires an inspection of the facility to ensure that it is equipped with the necessary fire safety equipment and has emergency evacuation plans in place.

Health department permit: A health department permit is required to ensure that your facility meets health and sanitation standards.

This permit is issued by the local health department and typically requires an inspection of the facility to ensure that it is clean, safe, and free from hazards.

Insurance: Liability insurance is required to protect your business from financial loss in the event of accidents or injuries. This insurance typically covers property damage and personal injury to customers, staff, and the dogs in your care.

Other licenses and permits: Depending on the location of your business, you may be required to obtain other licenses and permits, such as a sales tax permit or a food service permit.

It's important to research the specific licenses and permits required for your area and to apply for them well in advance of opening your business. It's also important to keep your licenses and permits current and to renew them as necessary.

In addition to obtaining licenses and permits, it's important to keep accurate records and to comply with all local, state, and federal regulations. This includes keeping records of vaccinations, health exams, and other veterinary care for the dogs in your care, as well as maintaining records of any incidents or accidents that occur at your facility.

In conclusion, obtaining licenses and permits is an important step in starting a dog boarding business. It's important to research the specific licenses and permits required for your area and to apply for them well in advance of opening your business. By keeping accurate records and complying with all local, state, and federal regulations, you can ensure that your business is operating legally and safely. Additionally, by ensuring that your facility has all the necessary permits, licenses, and insurance in place, you can provide a safe and healthy environment for the dogs in your care and for the staff.

When obtaining licenses and permits for your dog boarding business, it's important to also take into account the following additional details:

Check for local laws and regulations: Before starting your dog boarding business, check for any local laws and regulations that may apply to your business. This includes laws related to noise, waste management, and zoning.

Keep records: Keep accurate records of all licenses, permits, and inspections. This will help you stay organized and ensure that you are in compliance with all relevant regulations.

Inspections: Be prepared for inspections from local and state government agencies. These inspections will ensure that your facility is in compliance with all relevant regulations and that the welfare and safety of the dogs in your care are being met.

Insurance: Make sure you have adequate insurance to cover your business in case of accidents, injuries, or damage to the property. This will protect you and your business from financial loss.

Staff training: Train your staff on the proper procedures for obtaining licenses and permits and ensure that they understand the importance of compliance with all relevant regulations.

Stay informed: Stay informed of any changes to local laws and regulations that may affect your business. This will help you stay in compliance with all relevant regulations and avoid any potential legal issues.

By taking these additional details into account, you can ensure that your dog boarding business is fully compliant with all relevant laws and regulations. Additionally, by keeping accurate records, preparing for inspections, obtaining proper insurance, training staff and staying informed about any changes in regulations, you can minimize the risk of legal issues and ensure the safety and welfare of the dogs in your care.

Creating a Marketing Plan: Advertising and Promoting Your Business

Once your dog boarding business is up and running, it's important to create a marketing plan to attract customers and promote your business. A marketing plan is a detailed document that outlines how you will reach your target market, how you will promote your business, and how you will measure the success of your marketing efforts. Here are some steps to help you create an effective marketing plan for your dog boarding business:

Define your target market: The first step in creating a marketing plan is to define your target market. Your target market is the group of people who are most likely to use your services. When defining your target market, consider factors such as age, income, location, and interests.

Identify your unique selling points: Your unique selling points are the features and benefits of your business that set it apart from your competitors. Identify your unique selling points and use them to create a compelling message that will attract your target market.

Create a marketing budget: Create a marketing budget that outlines how much money you will spend on each marketing activity. Your marketing budget should be based on your target market, unique selling points, and overall business goals.

Develop a marketing mix: The marketing mix is the combination of marketing strategies and tactics that you will use to reach your target market. The marketing mix typically includes advertising, public relations, direct marketing, and personal selling.

Use social media: Social media is a powerful tool for promoting your business. Create a social media presence for your business and use it to engage with your target market, share information about your business, and promote your services.

Network: Networking is an effective way to promote your business. Attend networking events and join local business organizations to connect with other business owners and potential customers.

Use online marketing: Online marketing is an effective way to reach your target market. Use online marketing tools such as email marketing, search engine optimization (SEO), and pay-per-click advertising (PPC) to promote your business online.

Measure your results: It's important to measure the results of your marketing efforts to determine what's working and what's not. Use tools such as Google Analytics and social media analytics to track the success of your marketing efforts.

Offer promotions and discounts: Offering promotions and discounts is a great way to attract new customers and retain existing ones. Consider offering a special promotion for first-time customers, or a discount for repeat customers.

Get customer reviews and testimonials: Positive reviews and testimonials from satisfied customers can be a powerful marketing tool. Encourage your customers to leave reviews on your website, social media, or review sites.

Partner with other businesses: Partnering with other businesses can be a great way to promote your business. Consider partnering with a local pet store, dog groomer, or veterinarian to offer bundled services and cross-promote each other's businesses.

Host events: Hosting events such as open houses, meet and greets, or adoption events can be a great way to promote your business and connect with potential customers.

Volunteer and sponsor events: Volunteer and sponsor local events such as dog shows, charity walks, or pet fairs. This will give you an opportunity to connect with potential customers and promote your business.

By following these steps and implementing an effective marketing plan, you can attract new customers and promote your business. Additionally, by measuring the results of your marketing efforts, you can determine what strategies are working and make adjustments as needed. Remember to always be creative, think outside the box and be consistent in your efforts.

In conclusion, creating a marketing plan is an important step in promoting your dog boarding business. By defining your target market, identifying your unique selling points, creating a marketing budget, and using a variety of marketing strategies, you can effectively promote your business and attract new customers. Additionally, by measuring the results of your marketing efforts and making adjustments as needed, you can ensure that your marketing plan is effective and efficient.

Here are some additional details on creating a marketing plan for your dog boarding business:

Use visual marketing: Use visual marketing to promote your business, such as creating a website, business cards, brochures, and flyers. Visual marketing can be very effective in attracting potential customers and promoting your business.

Use email marketing: Email marketing can be an effective way to connect with potential customers and promote your business. Create an email list of potential customers and send them regular updates, promotions, and special offers.

Host contests and giveaways: Hosting contests and giveaways can be a great way to promote your business and attract new customers. Consider offering a prize such as a free night's stay at your facility or a gift basket filled with dog-related items.

Offer referral rewards: Encourage your current customers to refer their friends and family to your business by offering referral rewards. This can be a great way to attract new customers and promote your business.

Use video marketing: Video marketing can be a powerful tool for promoting your business. Create videos that showcase your facility, the services you offer, and the dogs in your care. Share these videos on your website, social media, and other online platforms.

Utilize Influencer marketing: Influencer marketing can be a powerful tool for promoting your business. Identify dog influencers on social media who have a large following and consider partnering with them to promote your business.

Create a loyalty program: Create a loyalty program for your customers. This will encourage them to come back to your business and can help you retain customers over time.

By implementing these additional details, you can create a comprehensive and effective marketing plan. Additionally, by using visual marketing, email marketing, hosting contests and giveaways, offering referral rewards, using video marketing, Influencer marketing and creating a loyalty program, you can reach a wider audience, increase brand awareness, and drive more business to your facility. Remember to always be creative, think outside the box, and be consistent in your efforts.

Hiring Staff: Finding the Right Team

When it comes to running a successful dog boarding business, one of the most important things you can do is to hire the right staff. The right team will help you provide top-notch care for the dogs in your care, manage the day-to-day operations of your business, and promote your business to potential customers. Here are some tips to help you find the right staff for your dog boarding business:

Define the roles and responsibilities: The first step in hiring staff is to define the roles and responsibilities of each position. This will help you determine the skills and qualifications that each position requires and make it easier to find the right candidate.

Create job descriptions: Create detailed job descriptions for each position. This will help you attract the right candidates and ensure that they understand the duties and expectations of the job.

Use online job postings: Use online job postings to reach a wider audience and attract more candidates. Websites such as Indeed, LinkedIn, and Glassdoor are great places to post job openings.

Utilize employee referrals: Employee referrals can be a great way to find talented candidates. Encourage your current staff to refer friends or family members who may be a good fit for the job.

Conduct thorough interviews: Once you have a pool of candidates, conduct thorough interviews to determine who is the best fit for the job. Ask a mix of behavioral and situational questions to get a sense of the candidate's qualifications and work style.

Check references and conduct background checks: Before making a job offer, check references and conduct background checks on the final candidates. This will help you verify the information provided by the candidate and ensure that the candidate is a good fit for the job.

Provide training and development: Once you've hired the right team, provide them with the training and development they need to succeed. This will help them provide the best care for the dogs in your care and promote your business to potential customers.

Create a positive work culture: Creating a positive work culture is essential for retaining staff. Encourage teamwork, provide opportunities for growth and development, and recognize and reward good performance.

Hiring the right staff for your dog boarding business is essential for the success of your business. By defining the roles and responsibilities, creating job descriptions, using online job postings, utilizing employee referrals, conducting thorough interviews, checking references and conducting background checks, providing training and development, creating a positive work culture, you can attract and retain the best staff for your business. This will help you provide top-notch care for the dogs in your care, manage the day-to-day operations of your business, and promote your business to potential customers.

Here are some additional details on hiring staff for your dog boarding business:

Look for candidates with experience and passion for animals: Ideally, you want to hire staff who have experience working with dogs, and who have a passion for animals. This will help ensure that they will provide the best care for the dogs in your care.

Check for certifications: Consider hiring staff who have certifications related to dog care, such as pet first aid, dog grooming, or dog behavior. This will give you an idea of their level of expertise and knowledge in caring for dogs.

Consider part-time and flexible schedules: Hiring part-time and flexible staff can be beneficial for your business. This will allow you to have a larger pool of staff to choose from, and will also make it easier to schedule staff based on the needs of your business.

Provide ongoing training and support: Once you've hired staff, it's important to provide ongoing training and support to ensure they have the knowledge and skills they need to provide the best care for the dogs in your care. This includes regular training sessions, online resources, and mentoring opportunities.

Evaluate performance: Regularly evaluate the performance of your staff and provide feedback. This will help them improve their skills, and also give you an idea of which staff members are excelling and which ones may need additional support.

Offer benefits: Offering benefits such as health insurance, retirement plans, and paid time off can help you attract and retain top talent.

By following these additional details, you can ensure that you are hiring the best staff for your dog boarding business. Additionally, by hiring staff with experience and passion for animals, checking for certifications, considering part-time and flexible schedules, providing ongoing training and support, evaluating performance and offering benefits you can help retain top talent and ensure that your staff is providing the best care for the dogs in your care, managing the day-to-day operations of your business, and promoting your business to potential customers.

Setting Rates and Policies: Establishing Your Business Structure

When starting a dog boarding business, it's important to establish your business structure and set rates and policies that will help you run your business effectively and profitably. Here are some tips to help you establish your business structure and set rates and policies for your dog boarding business:

Determine your business structure: The first step in establishing your business structure is to determine what type of business entity you want to be. You can choose to be a sole proprietorship, partnership, LLC, or corporation. Each type of business entity has its own advantages and disadvantages, so it's important to consult with a lawyer or accountant to determine which one is right for your business.

Set your rates: Setting your rates is a critical step in running a profitable business. You'll need to consider the cost of running your business, including the cost of food, supplies, and staff, when setting your rates. You'll also need to consider the rates of your competitors to ensure that your rates are competitive.

Establish policies: Establishing policies is an important step in running a successful business. You'll need to set policies for things like reservations, cancellations, and refunds, as well as policies for dealing with difficult customers.

Create a contract: Create a contract that outlines the terms and conditions of your services. This will help protect your business and ensure that your customers understand the terms of your services.

Establish a billing system: Establish a billing system that makes it easy for you to bill your customers and manage your finances. This can include setting up an online payment system or using a billing software.

Set up a customer management system: Setting up a customer management system can help you keep track of your customers and manage your reservations. This can include using a spreadsheet or a software program to manage your reservations and customer information.

Consider offering additional services: Offering additional services such as dog grooming, training, or transportation can help you increase your revenue and attract more customers.

Establishing your business structure, setting rates and policies, and creating a contract are critical steps in running a successful dog boarding business. Additionally, by considering your business costs, competitors' rates, creating policies, establishing a billing system, a customer management system and offering additional services, you will be able to manage your business effectively, attract more customers and increase revenue. By following these tips, you can ensure that your dog boarding business is profitable and successful.

Here are some additional details on setting rates and policies for your dog boarding business:

Understand your local market: Research the market in your area to understand the average rates for dog boarding. This will give you an idea of what you need to charge to be competitive.

Consider the type of service you provide: The type of service you provide can also affect your rates. For example, a luxury dog boarding facility will be able to charge higher rates than a basic facility.

Determine your occupancy rate: Determine your occupancy rate, which is the percentage of your facility that is occupied by dogs at any given time. This will help you determine how much you need to charge to cover your costs and make a profit.

Decide on the length of stay: Decide on the length of stay you will offer. Some dog boarding facilities only offer overnight stays, while others may offer longer stays. The length of stay you offer can also affect your rates.

Create a pricing structure: Create a pricing structure that takes into account the size of the dog, the length of stay, and any additional services offered. This will help you charge fair and competitive rates.

Establish refund and cancellation policies: Establish clear refund and cancellation policies that are fair to both you and your customers. This will help you manage last-minute cancellations and ensure that you are able to fill any empty spots.

Implement a pet policy: Implement a pet policy that outlines the rules and regulations for pet owners. This will help you ensure that all pets in your facility are well-behaved and that their owners understand your expectations.

Offer package deals: Offer package deals that include multiple services at a discounted rate. This will help you increase revenue and attract more customers.

By understanding your local market, considering the type of service you provide, determining your occupancy rate, deciding on the length of stay, creating a pricing structure, establishing refund and cancellation policies, implementing a pet policy, offering package deals, you can create a fair, competitive and attractive pricing structure for your dog boarding business. Additionally, by having a clear and fair pricing structure, you will be able to communicate your pricing to customers in a transparent and easy to understand way, which will make it easier for customers to make a decision about using your services.

Providing Quality Care: Meeting the Needs of Your Four-Legged Guests

When it comes to running a dog boarding business, providing quality care for your four-legged guests is of the utmost importance. Not only is it important for the well-being of the dogs in your care, but it will also help attract and retain customers. Here are some tips for providing quality care for your four-legged guests:

Conduct a thorough assessment of each dog: Before a dog stays at your facility, conduct a thorough assessment of each dog. This includes taking note of their medical history, dietary needs, and any special needs or behavior concerns. This information will help you provide the best care for each dog.

Create a comfortable and safe environment: Create a comfortable and safe environment for the dogs in your care. This includes providing a clean and comfortable living area, as well as ensuring that the facility is secure and free from hazards.

Provide plenty of exercise and playtime: Provide plenty of exercise and playtime for the dogs in your care. This will help keep them physically and mentally stimulated, and will also help them stay happy and healthy.

Provide proper nutrition: Provide proper nutrition for the dogs in your care. This includes providing a well-balanced diet and ensuring that each dog has access to fresh water at all times.

Provide regular grooming and hygiene care: Provide regular grooming and hygiene care for the dogs in your care. This includes bathing, brushing, and clipping nails. Regular grooming will help keep the dogs looking and feeling their best.

Provide regular medical care: Provide regular medical care for the dogs in your care. This includes administering medication as needed, and ensuring that each dog is up to date on their vaccinations.

Offer additional services: Offer additional services such as dog grooming, training, or transportation. This can help increase revenue and attract more customers.

Provide regular updates to owners: Provide regular updates to the owners of the dogs in your care. This will help keep them informed about the well-being of their dogs and will also help build trust and a positive relationship.

By conducting a thorough assessment of each dog, creating a comfortable and safe environment, providing plenty of exercise and playtime, proper nutrition, regular grooming and hygiene care, regular medical care, offer additional services and providing regular updates to owners, you can ensure that the dogs in your care are happy and healthy. Additionally, by providing quality care, you will be able to attract and retain customers, and will also be able to build a positive reputation in the community.

Here are some additional details on providing quality care for the dogs in your care:

Provide mental stimulation: Provide mental stimulation for the dogs in your care by providing interactive toys, puzzles and training sessions. This can help keep dogs happy and prevent boredom, which can lead to destructive behavior.

Monitor dogs for signs of stress: Be aware of the signs of stress in dogs, such as pacing, whining, or loss of appetite. If you notice any signs of stress, take steps to address the issue and make the dog more comfortable.

Have a plan for handling emergencies: Have a plan in place for handling emergencies such as illnesses or injuries. This should include having emergency contact information for the dogs' owners, as well as the contact information for a local vet.

Follow up with customers after their dog's stay: Follow up with customers after their dog's stay to see how their dog did and if they had any concerns or issues. This will help you address any problems, and also give you an opportunity to ask for feedback and improve your service.

Keep detailed records: Keep detailed records of each dog's stay, including their medical history, dietary needs, and any special needs or behavior concerns. This will help you provide better care and also help you to identify patterns and trends that may need to be addressed.

Take into account individual needs: Consider the individual needs of each dog in your care, such as age, size, breed, and temperament. This will help you provide the best care for each dog, and also help you to identify potential issues that may need to be addressed.

Create a daily routine: Create a daily routine for the dogs in your care, including feeding, exercise, and grooming. This will help keep the dogs in a routine, and also make it easier to identify any issues that may need to be addressed.

By considering these additional details, you can provide the best possible care for the dogs in your care. Additionally, by providing mental stimulation, monitoring dogs for signs of stress, having a plan for handling emergencies, following up with customers, keeping detailed records, taking into account individual needs

and creating a daily routine, you will be able to address any issues that may arise, provide a comfortable and safe environment, and ensure that the dogs in your care are happy and healthy.

Furthermore, it's important to have a good communication with the dog's owners, and make sure that they are aware of their dog's daily routine, and any issues or concerns that may arise. This will help you build trust and a positive relationship with your customers, and will also help you to identify any issues that may need to be addressed.

Also, make sure to keep your facility clean, hygienic and well-maintained, and ensure that the dogs have access to fresh water and clean bedding at all times. This will help keep the dogs healthy and comfortable, and also help prevent the spread of disease.

Additionally, it's important to be familiar with local and state laws and regulations regarding dog boarding, and ensure that your facility meets all of the necessary requirements. This includes obtaining necessary licenses and permits, as well as maintaining proper insurance coverage.

In conclusion, providing quality care for the dogs in your care is essential for the success of your dog boarding business. By conducting a thorough assessment of each dog, providing a comfortable and safe environment, providing plenty of exercise and playtime, proper nutrition, regular grooming and hygiene care, regular medical care, offering additional services, providing regular updates to owners, creating a daily routine, good communication with the dog's owners, keeping detailed records, taking into account individual needs, following local and state laws and regulations, keeping your facility clean and hygienic, and ensuring that dogs have access to fresh water and clean bedding, you can ensure that the dogs in your care are happy and healthy, and that your business is successful.

Keeping Accurate Records: Managing Your Finances

Managing your finances is a critical aspect of running a successful dog boarding business. Keeping accurate records can help you track your expenses, manage your cash flow, and make informed business decisions. Here are some tips for keeping accurate records and managing your finances for your dog boarding business:

Set up a system for tracking expenses: Set up a system for tracking expenses, such as using a spreadsheet or accounting software. This will help you keep track of your expenses and ensure that they are accurate.

Track your income: Track your income, including the amount of money you receive from boarding fees, additional services, and any other sources of income. This will help you understand your revenue and make informed business decisions.

Create a budget: Create a budget that takes into account your expenses and income. This will help you understand your financial situation and make informed business decisions.

Keep detailed records of your financial transactions: Keep detailed records of all financial transactions, including expenses, income, and any loans or investments. This will help you understand your financial situation and make informed business decisions.

Create financial reports: Create financial reports, such as profit and loss statements and balance sheets, to help you understand your financial situation and make informed business decisions.

Seek professional advice: Seek professional advice from an accountant or financial advisor to help you understand your financial situation and make informed business decisions.

Keep track of your tax obligations: Keep track of your tax obligations and ensure that you are paying your taxes on time. This will help you avoid any penalties or fines.

Have a plan for managing cash flow: Have a plan for managing cash flow, including managing expenses, managing accounts payable, and managing accounts receivable.

Here are some additional details on keeping accurate records and managing your finances for your dog boarding business:

Separate business and personal finances: It is important to keep your business finances separate from your personal finances. This will make it easier to track your expenses and income, and will also make it easier to file your taxes.

Automate financial processes: Automating financial processes, such as invoicing and payments, can help save time and reduce the risk of errors.

Monitor cash flow: Regularly monitor your cash flow to ensure that you have enough money coming in to cover your expenses. If you find that you are consistently running low on cash, you may need to adjust your pricing or find ways to increase your revenue.

Have a plan for unexpected expenses: Have a plan for unexpected expenses such as equipment repairs or emergencies. This can help you avoid financial stress and ensure that you are able to handle unexpected expenses.

Keep accurate records of inventory: Keep accurate records of inventory, including the cost of goods, the number of items in stock, and any sales. This will help you understand your costs and make informed decisions about inventory management.

Keep track of your loans: Keep track of any loans you have taken out, including the terms of the loan, the interest rate, and the repayment schedule. This will help you understand your financial obligations and make informed decisions about debt management.

Review your financial statements regularly: Review your financial statements regularly, including your income statement, balance sheet, and cash flow statement. This will help you understand your financial situation and make informed decisions about your business.

Use financial tools: Use financial tools such as budgeting and forecasting software, accounting software, and online invoicing and payment systems. This will help you to automate financial processes, save time, and reduce errors.

Additionally, by keeping accurate records of inventory, you can understand your costs and make informed decisions about inventory management, such as when to re-order items, what products are selling well and which aren't, and how to price your products. This information can be critical in making informed business decisions and improving your bottom line.

By keeping track of any loans you have taken out, you can understand your financial obligations and make informed decisions about debt management, such as when to pay off a loan, or when to consider taking out a new loan. This is important for maintaining a healthy financial situation and ensuring that your business is able to grow and expand over time.

Regularly reviewing your financial statements will give you a clear picture of your business's financial health, including your revenues, expenses, assets, and liabilities. This information can be critical in understanding your financial situation, and making informed decisions about your business.

Furthermore, using financial tools such as budgeting and forecasting software, accounting software, and online invoicing and payment systems can help automate financial processes, save time, and reduce errors. This can help you manage your finances more effectively and efficiently, and can also help you to make more informed business decisions.

In conclusion, keeping accurate records and managing your finances is an essential aspect of running a successful dog boarding business. By setting up a system for tracking expenses, tracking your income, creating a budget, keeping detailed records of your financial transactions, creating financial reports, seeking professional advice, keeping track of your tax obligations, having a plan for managing cash flow, separating business and personal finances, automating financial processes, monitoring cash flow, having a plan for unexpected expenses, keeping accurate records of inventory, keeping track of loans, reviewing your financial statements regularly, and using financial tools, you can better understand your financial situation, make informed business decisions, and ensure the long-term success of your dog boarding business.

Building Relationships: Networking with Other Pet Professionals

Networking with other pet professionals can be a valuable asset for your dog boarding business. By building relationships with other pet professionals, you can gain access to new customers, learn from experienced professionals, and stay current on industry trends. Here are some tips for building relationships with other pet professionals:

Attend industry events: Attend industry events such as pet trade shows, conferences, and workshops. This will give you the opportunity to meet other pet professionals and learn about the latest trends and developments in the industry.

Join professional organizations: Join professional organizations such as the National Association of Professional Pet Sitters or the International Boarding & Pet Services Association. These organizations provide networking opportunities, educational resources, and access to industry-specific information.

Collaborate with other pet professionals: Collaborate with other pet professionals such as dog trainers, groomers, and veterinarians. This can help you gain access to new customers and learn from experienced professionals.

Utilize social media: Utilize social media to connect with other pet professionals. Platforms like LinkedIn, Facebook and Instagram can be great ways to expand your professional network.

Build a referral network: Build a referral network with other pet professionals. This will give you the opportunity to refer customers to other pet professionals and also receive referrals from other pet professionals.

Share knowledge and expertise: Share knowledge and expertise with other pet professionals. This will help you build trust and establish yourself as an expert in the industry.

Be involved in the community: Be involved in your local pet-related community by volunteering, attending local events, and participating in pet-related organizations.

By attending industry events, joining professional organizations, collaborating with other pet professionals, utilizing social media, building a referral network, sharing knowledge and expertise, and being involved in the community, you can build relationships with other pet professionals and gain valuable insights into the industry. Additionally, by building a strong network of other pet professionals, you can gain access to new customers, learn from experienced professionals, and stay current on industry trends. This can ultimately help you grow your dog boarding business and increase your bottom line.

Here are some additional details on building relationships with other pet professionals:

Leverage your network to expand your reach: Leverage your network to expand your reach and gain new customers. For example, if you have a good relationship with a local dog trainer, you can ask them to recommend your services to their clients.

Offer to cross-promote services: Offer to cross-promote services with other pet professionals. For example, you can offer to include flyers for a local dog groomer in your customer welcome packet, and in return, they can include your business card in their grooming package.

Participate in local pet-related events: Participate in local pet-related events such as dog walks, adoption events, and pet-related charity events. This will give you the opportunity to network with other pet professionals, and also help you gain exposure for your business.

Consider offering internships or apprenticeships: Consider offering internships or apprenticeships to pet-related students or new professionals to help them gain experience and build their professional network.

Build relationships with local veterinarians: Building relationships with local veterinarians can help you stay informed about new medical developments and also help you provide better care for your four-legged guests.

Utilize online forums or message boards: Utilize online forums or message boards that are related to pet boarding industry, this can help you stay current on industry trends, ask questions, and connect with other pet professionals.

By leveraging your network to expand your reach, cross-promoting services, participating in local pet-related events, offering internships or apprenticeships, building relationships with local veterinarians and utilizing online forums or message boards, you can further strengthen your relationships with other pet professionals and gain valuable insights into the industry. Additionally, by expanding your network, you can gain access to new customers and opportunities to grow your business. Building relationships with other pet professionals is an ongoing process and requires consistency, but it's worth it as it can bring many benefits to your dog boarding business in the long run.

Keeping Up with Industry Trends: Staying Current in the Dog Boarding Business

Staying current on industry trends is important for the success of your dog boarding business. Keeping up with the latest developments in the dog boarding industry can help you stay competitive, attract new customers, and improve the quality of care you provide. Here are some tips for keeping up with industry trends in the dog boarding business:

Read industry publications: Read industry publications such as Pet Boarding & Daycare magazine, Pet Business, and Pet Groomer Magazine. These publications provide valuable information on the latest trends and developments in the industry.

Attend industry conferences and trade shows: Attend industry conferences and trade shows such as the Pet Boarding and Daycare Expo, and the International Boarding & Pet Services Association Conference. These events provide opportunities to learn about the latest trends, network with other professionals, and see new products and services.

Follow industry leaders on social media: Follow industry leaders on social media such as LinkedIn, Twitter, and Facebook. This will give you access to valuable information and insights on the latest trends and developments in the industry.

Join professional organizations: Join professional organizations such as the National Association of Professional Pet Sitters and the International Boarding & Pet Services Association. These organizations provide access to industry-specific information, educational resources, and networking opportunities.

Stay informed on new laws and regulations: Stay informed on new laws and regulations affecting the dog boarding industry. This will help you ensure that your business is in compliance with all local and state regulations.

Stay up to date on new technology and software: Stay up to date on new technology and software, such as online booking systems, and social media marketing tools, that can help streamline your business and improve customer service.

Continuously evaluate and improve your service: Continuously evaluate and improve your service, ask for feedback from your customers, and make changes to your service based on feedback. This can help you stay current with the latest customer trends and demands.

By reading industry publications, attending industry conferences and trade shows, following industry leaders on social media, joining professional organizations, staying informed on new laws and regulations, staying up to date on new technology and software and continuously evaluating and improving your service, you can stay current on industry trends and ensure the success of your dog boarding business. Additionally, by staying up to date on the latest trends, you can attract new customers, improve the quality of care you provide, and ensure that your business is in compliance with all local and state regulations. Staying current on industry trends is a continuous process and requires a commitment to learning, but it's worth it as it can bring many benefits to your dog boarding business in the long run.

Here are some additional details on keeping up with industry trends in the dog boarding business:

Develop a marketing strategy that incorporates the latest trends: Develop a marketing strategy that incorporates the latest trends in the industry, such as social media marketing and online advertising. This can help you reach new customers and stay competitive.

Offer new and innovative services: Offer new and innovative services such as doggy daycare, dog grooming, and dog training. This can help you stay current on industry trends and attract new customers.

Keep an eye on industry benchmarks: Keep an eye on industry benchmarks such as occupancy rates, average daily rate, and customer retention rate. This can help you understand your market position and make adjustments to your business strategy.

Take advantage of new technologies: Take advantage of new technologies such as GPS tracking, live streaming, and mobile apps. These technologies can help you provide better customer service, improve communication with clients, and stay competitive in the market.

Foster a culture of learning and improvement: Foster a culture of learning and improvement within your organization. Encourage your employees to attend industry events, read industry publications, and take advantage of online training opportunities. This can help you stay current on industry trends, and also help your employees improve their skills and knowledge.

Be open to change: Be open to change, and be willing to adapt to new trends, technologies, and customer preferences. This will help you stay current on industry trends and improve your service.

Offer a unique and personalized service: Offer a unique and personalized service that sets you apart from competitors. This can help you stay current on industry trends, and also attract new customers.

By developing a marketing strategy that incorporates the latest trends, offering new and innovative services, keeping an eye on industry benchmarks, taking advantage of new technologies, fostering a culture of learning and improvement, being open to change and offering a unique and personalized service, you can stay current on industry trends and ensure the success of your dog boarding business. Additionally, by staying up-to-date with the latest trends, you can improve your customer service, reach new customers, and stay competitive in the market. It's important to note that dog boarding industry is constantly evolving and it's crucial to stay informed and adapt to new trends, customer preferences, and technologies to run a successful dog boarding business.

Handling Emergencies: Preparing for the Unexpected

As a dog boarding business owner, it's important to be prepared for emergencies. By having a plan in place, you can ensure the safety of your guests, staff, and property. Here are some tips for handling emergencies and preparing for the unexpected:

Develop an emergency plan: Develop an emergency plan that includes procedures for evacuation, sheltering in place, and emergency communications. Train your staff on the emergency plan and conduct regular drills to ensure that everyone is prepared.

Have emergency equipment on hand: Have emergency equipment on hand such as fire extinguishers, first aid kits, and emergency lighting. Make sure that your staff knows where the equipment is located and how to use it.

Have an emergency contact list: Have an emergency contact list that includes contact information for your staff, local emergency services, and a veterinarian. Make sure that your staff knows how to access the list in case of an emergency.

Have a plan for severe weather: Have a plan for severe weather such as hurricanes, tornadoes, and snowstorms. This should include procedures for securing the facility, evacuating guests, and providing shelter for guests and staff.

Train your staff on emergency procedures: Train your staff on emergency procedures such as administering first aid, evacuating guests, and using emergency equipment. Make sure that your staff knows how to respond in case of an emergency.

Have an emergency fund: Have an emergency fund set aside to cover unexpected expenses such as emergency repairs or temporary boarding arrangements for guests.

Have an emergency plan for guests: Have an emergency plan for guests that includes procedures for emergency evacuation and emergency contact information. Make sure that your staff knows how to communicate this information to guests in case of an emergency.

Keep emergency contact information up-to-date: Keep emergency contact information up-to-date, including emergency contact information for guests, staff, and local emergency services.

By developing an emergency plan, having emergency equipment on hand, having an emergency contact list, having a plan for severe weather, training your staff on emergency procedures, having an emergency fund, having an emergency plan for guests and keeping emergency contact information up-to-date, you can ensure that you are prepared for emergencies and can respond quickly and effectively in case of an emergency. Additionally, by having a plan in place, you can ensure the safety of your guests, staff, and property, and minimize the potential impact of an emergency on your business. Preparing for the unexpected is a crucial aspect of running a dog boarding business, and it's important to regularly review and update your emergency plan to ensure that it stays current and effective.

Here are some additional details on handling emergencies and preparing for the unexpected in a dog boarding business:

Have a plan for contagious illnesses: Have a plan for contagious illnesses such as parvovirus, kennel cough, and distemper. This should include procedures for isolating sick guests, communicating with owners, and coordinating with a veterinarian.

Have a plan for medical emergencies: Have a plan for medical emergencies such as injuries, seizures, and allergic reactions. This should include procedures for administering first aid, contacting owners, and coordinating with a veterinarian.

Have a plan for power outages: Have a plan for power outages that includes procedures for providing emergency lighting, heating, and cooling. This should also include procedures for ensuring the safety of guests, staff, and property.

Have a plan for natural disasters: Have a plan for natural disasters such as floods, earthquakes, and wildfires. This should include procedures for evacuating guests, sheltering in place, and communicating with local emergency services.

Have a plan for security incidents: Have a plan for security incidents such as break-ins, theft, and vandalism. This should include procedures for contacting local emergency services, securing the facility, and protecting guests and staff.

Have a plan for staff injuries: Have a plan for staff injuries that includes procedures for administering first aid, contacting emergency services, and ensuring that injured staff receive proper medical attention.

Keep emergency supplies on hand: Keep emergency supplies on hand such as extra food, water, and bedding. This will ensure that you have the necessary supplies to take care of guests in case of an emergency.

Regularly review and update your emergency plan: Regularly review and update your emergency plan to ensure that it stays current and effective. This should be done at least once a year and after any significant changes to your business.

By having a plan for contagious illnesses, medical emergencies, power outages, natural disasters, security incidents, staff injuries, and keeping emergency supplies on hand, you can be prepared for any emergency that may arise in your dog boarding business. Additionally, by regularly reviewing and updating your emergency plan, you can ensure that it stays current and effective. Preparing for emergencies is crucial for the safety and well-being of your guests, staff, and property, and it's important to take the necessary steps to ensure that you are prepared for any unexpected situation.

Building a Strong Reputation: Managing Your Online Presence

In today's digital age, managing your online presence is crucial for the success of your dog boarding business. A strong online reputation can help you attract new customers, build trust with existing customers, and ultimately drive more business. Here are some tips for building a strong reputation and managing your online presence:

Claim and update your business listings: Claim and update your business listings on popular directories such as Google My Business, Yelp, and Facebook. This will ensure that your business information is accurate and up-to-date, and will also make it easier for customers to find you online.

Create a website: Create a website for your business that is professional and easy to navigate. This will provide potential customers with important information about your business such as services offered, rates, and contact information.

Use social media: Use social media platforms such as Facebook, Instagram, and Twitter to connect with customers and build your online presence. Share updates, photos, and videos of your business and guests to give customers a sense of what it's like to board their dog with you.

Encourage customer reviews: Encourage customers to leave reviews on popular review sites such as Yelp, Google, and Facebook. Positive reviews can help build trust with potential customers and also improve your search engine rankings.

Respond to customer reviews: Respond to customer reviews, both positive and negative. This will show that you value customer feedback and are committed to providing the best possible service.

Monitor your online reputation: Monitor your online reputation by setting up Google Alerts for your business name, and regularly searching for mentions of your business on social media. This will help you stay informed about what customers are saying about your business online.

Use SEO: Use SEO (Search Engine Optimization) techniques to improve your website's visibility on search engines. Use relevant keywords, meta tags, and backlinks to help improve your search engine rankings.

Offer excellent customer service: Offer excellent customer service and take care of the needs of your guests. This will help you build a positive reputation and attract new customers.

By claiming and updating your business listings, creating a website, using social media, encouraging customer reviews, responding to customer reviews, monitoring your online reputation, using SEO and offering excellent customer service, you can build a strong reputation and manage your online presence effectively. By managing your online reputation, you can attract new customers, build trust with existing customers, and ultimately drive more business to your dog boarding business. Building a strong reputation takes time and effort, but it's worth it as it can bring many benefits to your business in the long run.

Leverage customer testimonials: Use customer testimonials on your website and social media to showcase the positive experiences of your previous guests. This can help build trust with potential customers and showcase the value of your services.

Engage with your audience: Engage with your audience on social media by responding to comments and messages, and actively participating in online conversations. This can help build a community around your business and improve customer engagement.

Use high-quality images and videos: Use high-quality images and videos to showcase your facility, staff, and guests. This can help potential customers visualize what it's like to board their dog with you and can also help improve your search engine rankings.

Monitor your competition: Monitor your competition by keeping an eye on their online presence, marketing strategies, and customer reviews. This can help you identify areas where you can improve your own online presence and stay competitive in the market.

Address negative reviews promptly: Address negative reviews promptly by acknowledging the customer's concerns and addressing the issues. This can help mitigate the damage caused by negative reviews and show that you value customer feedback.

Use analytics: Use analytics tools such as Google Analytics to track the performance of your website and social media channels. This can help you understand how customers are engaging with your business online and identify areas for improvement.

By leveraging customer testimonials, engaging with your audience, using high-quality images and videos, monitoring your competition, addressing negative reviews promptly, and using analytics, you can build a strong reputation and manage your online presence effectively. Additionally, by monitoring your online reputation and staying active on social media, you can create a community around your business, improve customer engagement, and showcase the value of your services. Building a strong reputation is not just about attracting new customers but also about maintaining existing customers and creating a positive image of your business.

Offering Additional Services: Expanding Your Business

Offering additional services can be a great way to expand your dog boarding business and increase revenue. By providing a variety of services, you can attract new customers, retain existing customers, and differentiate yourself from your competitors. Here are some tips for offering additional services and expanding your business:

- Identify your target market: Identify your target market and determine what additional services they may be interested in. This can include services such as dog grooming, dog training, and doggy daycare.

- Conduct market research: Conduct market research to determine the demand for the additional services you are considering. This can include surveying current customers, conducting online research, and talking to other pet professionals in your area.

- Invest in equipment and training: Invest in equipment and training to provide additional services. This can include buying grooming tables and clippers for dog grooming, or hiring a dog trainer to provide training classes.

- Develop a pricing strategy: Develop a pricing strategy that is competitive and will generate a profit. This can include charging by the hour or session for additional services, or offering package deals for multiple services.

- Promote your additional services: Promote your additional services through your website, social media, and traditional marketing methods. This can include creating flyers, brochures and special promotions to attract new customers to your additional services.

- Provide excellent customer service: Provide excellent customer service for your additional services, just as you do for your dog boarding services. This can include being responsive to customer needs, providing a detailed service menu, and offering a satisfaction guarantee.

- Create a schedule: Create a schedule for your additional services that works well for both your staff and your customers. This can include offering services during peak hours, and having a backup staff in case of unexpected demand.

- Continuously evaluate and improve: Continuously evaluate and improve your additional services by collecting customer feedback and making changes as needed. This can help you to identify what your customers want and what services are most profitable for your business.

By identifying your target market, conducting market research, investing in equipment and training, developing a pricing strategy, promoting your additional services, providing excellent customer service, creating a schedule, and continuously evaluating and improving your additional services, you can successfully expand your dog boarding business and increase revenue. Additionally, by offering a variety of services, you can attract new customers, retain existing customers, and differentiate yourself from your competitors. Remember, it's important to be flexible and adapt to the changing demands of your customers. Expanding your business can come with its own set of challenges but with the right strategy and execution, it can bring many benefits to your business in the long run.

- Offer package deals: Offer package deals for your additional services, such as a dog grooming and dog training package. This can help attract customers who are looking for a one-stop-shop for their pet's needs and can also increase revenue.

- Partner with other pet professionals: Partner with other pet professionals in your area, such as veterinarians, dog walkers, or pet supply stores. This can help you to expand your services, increase your reach, and build your reputation in the community.

- Utilize online booking: Utilize online booking for your additional services, which allows customers to easily book and pay for services online. This can make it more convenient for customers and increase bookings.

- Create a loyalty program: Create a loyalty program for your additional services, which rewards customers for repeat business. This can help to retain existing customers and increase revenue.

- Offer pick-up and delivery services: Offer pick-up and delivery services for your additional services, which can be a convenience for customers who are unable to drop off and pick up their pet.

- Offer a mobile service: Offer a mobile service, where you can provide additional services such as dog grooming, at the customer's home. This can be an additional revenue stream, as well as a convenience for customers who are unable to transport their pet to your facility.

By offering package deals, partnering with other pet professionals, utilizing online booking, creating a loyalty program, offering pick-up and delivery services, and offering a mobile service, you can expand your dog boarding business and increase revenue. Additionally, by continuously evaluating and improving your additional services, you can ensure that you are meeting the needs of your customers and staying competitive in the market. Remember, it's important to keep in mind that the key to a successful expansion is to understand the needs and wants of your customers, and to offer services that they are willing to pay for.

Providing Training and Education: Advancing Your Skills and Knowledge

Providing training and education is an important aspect of running a successful dog boarding business. By continuing to learn and advance your skills and knowledge, you can provide better care for your guests, improve customer satisfaction, and stay competitive in the market. Here are some tips for providing training and education and advancing your skills and knowledge:

- Stay current on industry trends: Stay current on industry trends by reading pet-related publications, attending conferences and seminars, and participating in online forums. This can help you to stay up-to-date on the latest practices and technologies, and to learn about new products and services.
- Take advantage of online resources: Take advantage of online resources such as webinars, podcasts, and blogs to learn about new trends, best practices, and industry standards. This can help you to learn from experts in the field and stay current on industry developments.
- Invest in professional development: Invest in professional development by taking courses, workshops, and certifications that are relevant to your business. This can help you to improve your skills, stay current on industry standards, and gain credibility in the market.
- Provide training for your staff: Provide training for your staff on industry trends, best practices, and industry standards. This can help your staff to provide better care for your guests and improve customer satisfaction.

- Network with other pet professionals: Network with other pet professionals in your area, such as veterinarians, dog trainers, and pet supply store owners. This can help you to learn from others in the field, gain new perspectives, and expand your professional network.
- Learn about canine behavior: Learn about canine behavior by taking courses and workshops, and reading books on the subject. This can help you to understand the needs of your guests and provide better care for them.
- Keep accurate records: Keep accurate records of your training and education, including certificates, workshop materials, and notes. This can help you to document your knowledge and skills, and to demonstrate your commitment to professional development.
- Seek out mentorship opportunities: Seek out mentorship opportunities with experienced and successful dog boarding business owners. This can provide you with valuable advice, guidance, and industry insights that can help you to improve your business.
- Attend networking events: Attend networking events, such as pet industry trade shows, to meet other pet professionals, learn about new products and services, and gain new perspectives on the industry.
- Volunteer or intern: Volunteer or intern at local animal shelters or rescue organizations to gain hands-on experience working with dogs and learn about different breeds, behaviors, and health concerns.
- Specialize in a specific area: Specialize in a specific area of the dog boarding business, such as caring for senior dogs or providing services for dogs with special needs.

This can help you to differentiate yourself in the market and attract a specific niche of customers.

- Stay up-to-date on regulations: Stay up-to-date on regulations and laws that pertain to the dog boarding industry. This can help you to ensure that your business is in compliance with local, state, and federal regulations, and to avoid any legal issues.
- Provide continuing education for your staff: Provide continuing education for your staff to ensure they are knowledgeable and current on the latest industry trends, best practices, and regulations. This can help your staff to provide better care for your guests, and improve customer satisfaction.

By staying current on industry trends, taking advantage of online resources, investing in professional development, providing training for your staff, networking with other pet professionals, learning about canine behavior and keeping accurate records, you can advance your skills and knowledge and run a successful dog boarding business. Additionally, by continuing to learn and improve, you can provide better care for your guests, improve customer satisfaction, and stay competitive in the market. Remember, providing training and education is an ongoing process and it's important to make it a priority in your business. By staying up-to-date with the latest trends, and staying informed of best practices, you can ensure that you are providing the best possible service to your customers.

Maintaining a Safe and Clean Environment: Implementing Health and Safety Procedures

Maintaining a safe and clean environment is essential for running a successful dog boarding business. By implementing health and safety procedures, you can provide a comfortable and healthy environment for your guests, improve customer satisfaction, and protect your business from potential liabilities. Here are some tips for maintaining a safe and clean environment and implementing health and safety procedures:

- Develop a cleaning and disinfection protocol: Develop a cleaning and disinfection protocol that includes regular cleaning and disinfection of all surfaces and equipment, as well as regular laundry and bedding changes. This can help to prevent the spread of disease and ensure that your facility is clean and sanitary.
- Implement a pest control program: Implement a pest control program that includes regular inspections, treatments, and preventative measures to control pests such as fleas, ticks, and rodents. This can help to maintain a healthy environment for your guests and protect your business from potential liabilities.
- Conduct regular health checks: Conduct regular health checks on your guests to ensure that they are healthy and free from any contagious diseases. This can help to prevent the spread of disease among your guests and protect your business from potential liabilities.
- Implement a vaccination policy: Implement a vaccination policy that requires all guests to be up-to-date on their vaccinations. This can help to protect your guests and your business from potential liabilities.

- Create emergency protocols: Create emergency protocols for dealing with fires, natural disasters, power outages, and other emergencies. This can help to protect your guests and your business in the event of an emergency.
- Train your staff: Train your staff on health and safety procedures, including cleaning and disinfection, pest control, health checks, and emergency protocols. This can ensure that your staff is knowledgeable and capable of maintaining a safe and clean environment.
- Regularly review and update: Regularly review and update your health and safety procedures to ensure that they are up-to-date and effective. This can help to ensure that your facility is safe and clean for your guests and can reduce the risk of liabilities.
- Implement fire safety measures: Implement fire safety measures such as fire alarms, smoke detectors, and fire extinguishers. Conduct regular fire drills to ensure that your staff is prepared to handle an emergency situation. This can help to protect your guests and your business in the event of a fire.
- Maintain proper ventilation: Maintain proper ventilation in your facility to ensure that the air is fresh and clean. This can help to prevent the spread of disease and ensure that your guests are comfortable.
- Keep the facility well-lit: Keep the facility well-lit to ensure that your guests can see and move around safely. This can help to prevent accidents and injuries.
- Provide appropriate bedding: Provide appropriate bedding for your guests, such as comfortable beds and blankets. This can help to ensure that your guests are comfortable and can improve customer satisfaction.

- Keep the facility secure: Keep the facility secure to ensure that your guests are safe. This can include installing security cameras, alarm systems, and locks.
- Assign a staff member to monitor the facility: Assign a staff member to monitor the facility and ensure that the guests are safe and comfortable. This can help to prevent accidents and injuries and ensure that your guests are well-cared for.
- Be prepared for emergencies: Be prepared for emergencies by having emergency contact information and emergency medical supplies on hand. This can help to ensure that your guests are safe and can improve customer satisfaction.

By implementing fire safety measures, maintaining proper ventilation, keeping the facility well-lit, providing appropriate bedding, keeping the facility secure, assigning a staff member to monitor the facility, and being prepared for emergencies, you can maintain a safe and clean environment for your guests and improve customer satisfaction. Additionally, by implementing these procedures, you can protect your business from potential liabilities and ensure that your business is in compliance with industry standards. Remember, maintaining a safe and clean environment is an ongoing process, it's important to make it a priority in your business, and to stay informed and educated about industry standards, best practices and regulations.

Providing a Home-Like Experience: Creating a Comfortable Atmosphere

Providing a home-like experience is essential for running a successful dog boarding business. By creating a comfortable atmosphere, you can provide a welcoming and relaxed environment for your guests, improve customer satisfaction, and attract repeat customers. Here are some tips for providing a home-like experience and creating a comfortable atmosphere:

- Create a warm and welcoming environment: Create a warm and welcoming environment by decorating your facility with comfortable furniture, artwork, and plants. This can help to create a relaxed and inviting atmosphere for your guests.
- Provide a variety of activities: Provide a variety of activities for your guests such as toys, puzzles, and games. This can help to keep your guests entertained and engaged, and can improve customer satisfaction.
- Create a personalized experience: Create a personalized experience by getting to know your guests, and providing individualized care and attention. This can help to make your guests feel more at home, and can improve customer satisfaction.
- Provide comfortable sleeping arrangements: Provide comfortable sleeping arrangements for your guests, such as cozy beds and blankets. This can help to ensure that your guests are comfortable and can improve customer satisfaction.
- Offer a variety of amenities: Offer a variety of amenities such as grooming services, playtime, and training

classes. This can help to provide a comprehensive experience for your guests, and can improve customer satisfaction.

- Foster a sense of community: Foster a sense of community by hosting events such as meet-and-greets, and encouraging your guests to interact with each other. This can help to create a social atmosphere, and can improve customer satisfaction.
- Provide a sense of security: Provide a sense of security by making sure that your facility is well-lit, secure, and monitored. This can help to ensure that your guests are safe and can improve customer satisfaction.
- Provide natural light: Provide natural light by installing large windows, skylights, or sun tunnels. This can help to create a bright and open atmosphere and can help to boost the mood and well-being of your guests.
- Incorporate nature: Incorporate nature by adding plants, trees, or even a small garden in your facility. This can help to create a calm and relaxing atmosphere and can help to reduce stress and anxiety in your guests.
- Incorporate soothing colors: Incorporate soothing colors such as pale blue, green, and yellow in your facility. These colors can help to create a calm and relaxing atmosphere and can help to reduce stress and anxiety in your guests.
- Create separate spaces: Create separate spaces such as play areas, sleeping areas, and quiet areas. This can help to provide a sense of privacy and can help to create a comfortable and relaxing atmosphere for your guests.
- Use comfortable and durable materials: Use comfortable and durable materials such as soft fabrics, carpeting, and sturdy furniture in your facility. This can help to create a comfortable and relaxing atmosphere

for your guests and can help to ensure that your facility is durable and easy to maintain.

- Use calming scents: Use calming scents such as lavender, vanilla, or peppermint in your facility. This can help to create a relaxing atmosphere and can help to reduce stress and anxiety in your guests.
- Provide a sense of familiarity: Provide a sense of familiarity by allowing your guests to bring their own bedding, toys, or other personal items. This can help to create a sense of home and can help to reduce stress and anxiety in your guests.

By providing natural light, incorporating nature, incorporating soothing colors, creating separate spaces, using comfortable and durable materials, using calming scents, and providing a sense of familiarity, you can create a comfortable and relaxing atmosphere for your guests and improve customer satisfaction. Additionally, by providing a home-like experience, you can attract repeat customers and build a loyal customer base. Remember, providing a home-like experience is an ongoing process, it's important to make it a priority in your business, and to constantly look for ways to improve and enhance the experience for your guests.

Building Repeat Business: Retaining Customers

Building repeat business is essential for running a successful dog boarding business. By retaining customers, you can improve customer satisfaction, increase revenue, and grow your business. Here are some tips for building repeat business and retaining customers:

- Provide excellent customer service: Provide excellent customer service by being friendly, responsive, and accommodating your guests' needs. This can help to improve customer satisfaction, and can encourage customers to return.
- Follow up with customers: Follow up with customers after their stay to ask for feedback and address any concerns. This can help to improve customer satisfaction, and can encourage customers to return.
- Offer loyalty programs: Offer loyalty programs such as discounts or rewards for repeat customers. This can encourage customers to return, and can improve customer satisfaction.
- Keep in touch with customers: Keep in touch with customers through email, social media, or newsletters. This can help to build a relationship with your customers, and can encourage customers to return.
- Offer special promotions or events: Offer special promotions or events such as holiday or seasonal specials. This can encourage customers to return and can improve customer satisfaction.
- Build a relationship with your customers: Build a relationship with your customers by getting to know

their pets, their likes, and dislikes. This can help to create a personalized experience and can encourage customers to return.

- Keep your business updated: Keep your business updated by staying informed about industry trends and best practices. This can help to improve customer satisfaction and can encourage customers to return.
- Offer flexible booking options: Offer flexible booking options such as online booking, last-minute booking, and long-term booking. This can help to accommodate the needs of your customers, and can encourage customers to return.
- Use customer feedback to improve: Use customer feedback to improve your services and address any issues or concerns. This can help to improve customer satisfaction and can encourage customers to return.
- Keep accurate records: Keep accurate records of your customers' preferences, allergies, and other important information. This can help to provide a personalized experience and can encourage customers to return.
- Build trust with your customers: Build trust with your customers by being transparent and upfront about your policies, procedures, and prices. This can help to build a relationship with your customers and can encourage customers to return.
- Offer pick-up and drop-off services: Offer pick-up and drop-off services for your customers. This can help to accommodate the needs of your customers, and can encourage customers to return.
- Create a sense of community: Create a sense of community by hosting events such as meet-and-greets, and encouraging your customers to interact with each

other. This can help to build a relationship with your customers and can encourage customers to return.

- Keep your facility clean and well-maintained: Keep your facility clean and well-maintained to ensure that your customers' pets are safe and comfortable. This can help to improve customer satisfaction and can encourage customers to return.

By offering flexible booking options, using customer feedback to improve, keeping accurate records, building trust with your customers, offering pick-up and drop-off services, creating a sense of community, and keeping your facility clean and well-maintained, you can build repeat business and retain customers. Additionally, by providing a positive and welcoming experience, you can attract new customers and grow your business. Remember, building repeat business is an ongoing process, it's important to make it a priority in your business, and to constantly look for ways to improve and enhance the experience for your customers.

Handling Difficult Situations: Dealing with Complaints and Issues

Handling difficult situations is an inevitable part of running a dog boarding business. By dealing with complaints and issues effectively, you can improve customer satisfaction, maintain a positive reputation, and protect your business. Here are some tips for handling difficult situations and dealing with complaints and issues:

- Listen actively: Listen actively to your customers and try to understand their concerns. This can help to diffuse the situation and can help to improve customer satisfaction.
- Apologize and take responsibility: Apologize and take responsibility for any mistakes or issues that may have occurred. This can help to build trust with your customers and can help to improve customer satisfaction.
- Offer a solution: Offer a solution to the problem, such as a refund, discount, or compensation. This can help to improve customer satisfaction and can help to resolve the issue.
- Follow up with your customers: Follow up with your customers to ensure that the problem has been resolved and that they are satisfied with the solution. This can help to build trust with your customers and can help to improve customer satisfaction.
- Learn from your mistakes: Learn from your mistakes and take steps to prevent similar issues from occurring in the future. This can help to improve customer satisfaction and can help to protect your business.

- Train your staff to handle difficult situations: Train your staff to handle difficult situations and to provide excellent customer service. This can help to improve customer satisfaction and can help to protect your business.
- Have a plan in place: Have a plan in place for dealing with complaints and issues, and make sure that your staff is aware of the plan. This can help to improve customer satisfaction and can help to protect your business.
- Be prepared to handle emergencies: Be prepared to handle emergencies such as a medical emergency with a pet or unexpected weather conditions. Have a plan in place and make sure that your staff is trained on how to handle these situations. This can help to ensure the safety of your guests and can help to protect your business.
- Be transparent: Be transparent and honest with your customers about any issues or concerns that may arise during their pet's stay. This can help to build trust with your customers and can help to improve customer satisfaction.
- Communicate effectively: Communicate effectively with your customers and staff. This can help to resolve issues more quickly and can help to prevent misunderstandings.
- Be proactive: Be proactive by regularly checking in on your guests and addressing any issues or concerns that may arise. This can help to improve customer satisfaction and can help to protect your business.
- Keep your cool: Keep your cool and remain calm during difficult situations. This can help to diffuse the situation and can help to improve customer satisfaction.

- Be empathetic: Be empathetic and try to understand your customers' perspective. This can help to improve customer satisfaction and can help to resolve issues more quickly.
- Document everything: Document everything, including customer complaints, issues, and resolutions. This can help to track trends, identify patterns, and can help to prevent similar issues from happening in the future.

By being prepared for emergencies, being transparent, communicating effectively, being proactive, keeping your cool, being empathetic, and documenting everything, you can handle difficult situations effectively and improve customer satisfaction. Additionally, by dealing with complaints and issues quickly and efficiently, you can maintain a positive reputation and protect your business. Remember, handling difficult situations is an ongoing process, it's important to make it a priority in your business, and to constantly look for ways to improve and enhance your customer service.

Insurance and Liability: Protecting Your Business

Insurance and liability are essential for running a dog boarding business. By having the proper insurance and understanding your liability, you can protect your business, your assets, and your customers. Here are some tips for insurance and liability:

- Understand your liability: Understand your liability as a dog boarding business. This includes understanding the laws, regulations, and requirements for your state and local area. It also includes understanding your responsibilities as a business owner and how to protect yourself and your business from potential lawsuits.
- Get the right insurance: Get the right insurance for your dog boarding business. This includes liability insurance, which covers damages or injuries caused by your business or your employees. It also includes property insurance, which covers damages to your facility and equipment. And it includes worker's compensation insurance to cover employees injured while working.
- Understand your policy: Understand your policy, including what is covered and what is not covered. This includes understanding any exclusions or limitations, and how to file a claim if you need to.
- Review your insurance regularly: Review your insurance regularly, and update your coverage as needed. This includes reviewing your liability coverage, your property coverage, and any other insurance you may have.
- Have a plan in case of emergency: Have a plan in case of emergency, such as a natural disaster or a medical emergency. This plan should include evacuation

procedures, emergency contact information, and emergency supplies.

- Train your staff: Train your staff on emergency procedures and on how to handle potential liability issues. This can help to protect your business and your employees.

when it comes to understanding your liability as a dog boarding business, it is important to be aware of the laws and regulations that pertain to your industry. This may include understanding zoning laws and regulations, animal welfare laws, and health and safety regulations. Additionally, it is important to have a clear understanding of your responsibilities as a business owner, including your responsibility to provide a safe and healthy environment for the dogs in your care, as well as your responsibility to the customers who entrust their pets to you.

When it comes to getting the right insurance for your dog boarding business, it is important to consider the specific needs of your business. Liability insurance is essential to protect you from financial loss in case of accidents or injuries caused by your business or your employees. Property insurance is also important to protect your facility and equipment in case of damage or loss. And worker's compensation insurance is important to cover employees injured while working.

It's important to understand the coverage of your policy and what is covered and what is not covered. This includes understanding any exclusions or limitations, as well as understanding how to file a claim if you need to.

Additionally, it is important to review your insurance regularly and update your coverage as needed. This may include increasing your liability coverage as your business grows, or updating your property coverage to reflect any changes to your facility or equipment.

Having a plan in case of emergency is also important. This plan should include evacuation procedures, emergency contact information, and emergency supplies. Training your staff on emergency procedures and on how to handle potential liability issues can help to protect your business and your employees.

It's also important to have a good understanding of how to handle and respond to any complaints or disputes. This includes understanding how to handle difficult situations and how to communicate effectively with your customers. It's also important to document everything, including customer complaints, issues, and resolutions, in order to track trends, identify patterns and prevent similar issues from happening in the future.

By understanding your liability, getting the right insurance, understanding your policy, reviewing your insurance regularly, having a plan in case of emergency and training your staff, you can protect your business and ensure that you and your employees are covered in case of an accident or incident. Additionally, by being aware of your liabilities, you can take proactive steps to reduce your risk and maintain a safe environment for your guests. Remember, protecting your business is an ongoing process, it's important to make it a priority in your business, and to constantly look for ways to improve and enhance your liability coverage.

Building a Strong Website: Creating an Online Presence

Creating a strong website is essential for any business, including a dog boarding business. A website is often the first point of contact between a potential customer and your business. A well-designed and informative website can help to attract new customers, establish your business as a professional and credible provider of dog boarding services, and help to build trust with your customers. Here are some tips for building a strong website:

- Make it easy to navigate: Make it easy for visitors to navigate your website. This includes having a clear and intuitive menu structure, and providing links to important pages such as your contact page, rates and policies, and frequently asked questions.
- Include high-quality images: Include high-quality images of your facility, your staff, and the dogs in your care. Images can help to attract new customers and help to build trust with your customers.
- Provide detailed information: Provide detailed information about your services, including your rates, policies, and procedures. This can help to attract new customers and help to build trust with your customers.
- Make it mobile-friendly: Make sure that your website is mobile-friendly, so that it can be easily accessed on a smartphone or tablet. This can help to attract new customers and help to build trust with your customers.
- Include customer reviews: Include customer reviews on your website. This can help to attract new customers and help to build trust with your customers.

- Make it easy to contact you: Make it easy for visitors to contact you. This includes providing a contact form, an email address, and a phone number.
- Optimize your website for search engines: Optimize your website for search engines, including including keywords and meta tags, which can help to improve your search engine rankings and make it easier for potential customers to find your website.

In addition to the tips mentioned above, there are a few more things to consider when building a strong website for your dog boarding business.

- Make it visually appealing: Your website should be visually appealing and professional looking. This includes using high-quality graphics and images, as well as a clean and modern design. This can help to attract new customers and make a positive first impression.
- Use clear and concise language: Use clear and concise language when describing your services and policies. This can help to attract new customers and help to build trust with your customers.
- Keep it updated: Keep your website updated with current information about your services, rates, policies, and procedures. This can help to attract new customers and help to build trust with your customers.
- Include a blog or news section: Include a blog or news section on your website. This can help to attract new customers and help to build trust with your customers. A blog can be used to share information about your business, including updates, news, and tips on how to take care of dogs.

- Include a calendar of events: Include a calendar of events on your website. This can help to attract new customers and help to build trust with your customers. A calendar of events can be used to share information about upcoming events, such as training classes, meet and greets, and other activities.
- Include a FAQ page: Include a FAQ page on your website. This can help to attract new customers and help to build trust with your customers. A FAQ page can be used to share information about your services, rates, policies, and procedures, and can also be used to answer common questions about your business.

By making your website visually appealing, using clear and concise language, keeping it updated, including a blog or news section, including a calendar of events, and including a FAQ page, you can provide a comprehensive and informative website that can help to attract new customers, establish your business as a professional and credible provider of dog boarding services, and help to build trust with your customers. Additionally, by keeping your website updated and providing valuable information, you can also establish yourself as a valuable resource for pet owners and dog lovers. Remember, building a strong website is an ongoing process, it's important to make it a priority in your business, and to constantly look for ways to improve and enhance your website.

Utilizing Social Media: Connecting with Customers

Utilizing social media is an essential part of building and promoting your dog boarding business. Social media platforms such as Facebook, Instagram, and Twitter can help to attract new customers, build relationships with existing customers, and promote your services. Here are some tips for utilizing social media for your dog boarding business:

- Choose the right platforms: Choose the right platforms for your business. This includes platforms that your target audience is likely to use, such as Facebook and Instagram.
- Create a consistent brand: Create a consistent brand across all of your social media platforms. This includes using the same profile picture and cover photo, and the same tone of voice.
- Share high-quality content: Share high-quality content on your social media platforms. This includes pictures and videos of your facility, your staff, and the dogs in your care. It also includes information about your services, rates, and policies.
- Engage with your followers: Engage with your followers on your social media platforms. This includes responding to comments and messages, and sharing user-generated content.
- Use hashtags: Use hashtags to make your content more discoverable. This includes using industry-specific hashtags, as well as more general hashtags such as #dogboarding and #petcare.

- Run social media promotions: Run social media promotions, such as contests and giveaways, to attract new customers and build relationships with existing customers.
- Keep track of your metrics: Keep track of your metrics, such as likes, shares, and comments, to better understand the success of your social media efforts.

In addition to the tips mentioned above, there are a few more things to consider when utilizing social media for your dog boarding business.

- Use the platforms to tell your story: Use social media platforms to tell your story, including the story of your business, your staff, and the dogs in your care. Share behind-the-scenes photos and videos, as well as information about your services and philosophy.
- Use social media to build trust: Use social media platforms to build trust with your customers. Share customer testimonials and reviews, as well as photos and videos of happy dogs in your care.
- Use social media to offer special deals and discounts: Use social media platforms to offer special deals and discounts to your followers. This can include discounts for repeat customers, or special deals for customers who book online.
- Use social media to educate: Use social media platforms to educate your followers. Share information about dog care, training, and behavior, as well as information about your services and policies.
- Use social media to create a sense of community: Use social media platforms to create a sense of community among your followers. This can include hosting online

meet-ups, creating a private Facebook group for customers, or hosting online events.

- Use social media to listen: Use social media platforms to listen to your customers. This includes monitoring your social media accounts for comments and messages, and responding to customer feedback.

By using social media to tell your story, build trust, offer special deals and discounts, educate, create a sense of community and listen, you can attract new customers, build relationships with existing customers, and promote your services on social media. Additionally, by using social media to educate and offer special deals, you can also establish yourself as a valuable resource for pet owners and dog lovers. Remember, utilizing social media is an ongoing process, it's important to make it a priority in your business, and to constantly look for ways to improve and enhance your social media presence.

Creating a Strong Brand: Developing Your Business Identity

Creating a strong brand is essential for any business, including a dog boarding business. A strong brand can help to attract new customers, establish your business as a professional and credible provider of dog boarding services, and help to build trust with your customers. Here are some tips for creating a strong brand for your dog boarding business:

- Define your brand: Define your brand by identifying your unique selling points, values, and mission statement. This can help to attract new customers and help to build trust with your customers.
- Create a logo and tagline: Create a logo and tagline that represents your brand. This includes a visual representation of your business, such as a logo, and a short phrase that represents your business, such as a tagline. This can help to attract new customers and help to build trust with your customers.
- Develop a consistent visual style: Develop a consistent visual style for your brand. This includes using the same colors, font, and imagery across all of your marketing materials. This can help to attract new customers and help to build trust with your customers.
- Use your brand in all of your marketing materials: Use your brand in all of your marketing materials, including your website, business cards, brochures, and flyers. This can help to attract new customers and help to build trust with your customers.
- Communicate your brand: Communicate your brand through your website, social media, and other

marketing materials. This can help to attract new customers and help to build trust with your customers.

- Be consistent: Be consistent in the way you present your brand. This includes using the same colors, font, and imagery across all of your marketing materials, as well as using the same tone of voice in your communications.
- Protect your brand: Protect your brand by registering your business name, logo, and tagline as trademarks, and by monitoring the use of your brand on social media and the internet.

In addition to the tips mentioned above, there are a few more things to consider when creating a strong brand for your dog boarding business.

- Be authentic: Be authentic in your branding. This means being true to who you are as a business and what you stand for. This will help to attract customers who are looking for a business that aligns with their values.
- Tell your story: Tell your story through your branding. Share information about the history of your business, the people behind it, and the passion that drives it. This will help to create a connection with customers and make your brand more relatable.
- Use brand storytelling: Use brand storytelling to create an emotional connection with your customers. Use your website, social media, and other marketing materials to share personal anecdotes, inspiring stories, and relatable content.
- Use customer testimonials: Use customer testimonials in your branding. Share positive feedback from customers on your website, social media, and other

marketing materials. This can help to build trust and attract new customers.

- Create a brand voice: Create a brand voice that is consistent across all of your communications. This includes the tone of voice used in your website, social media, and other marketing materials. This will help to create a consistent image for your brand.
- Stay true to your brand: Stay true to your brand. This means being consistent in the way you present your brand, and not straying from your core values. This will help to build trust with customers and establish your business as a credible provider of dog boarding services.

By being authentic, telling your story, using brand storytelling, using customer testimonials, creating a brand voice and staying true to your brand, you can create a strong brand that will help to attract new customers, establish your business as a professional and credible provider of dog boarding services, and help to build trust with your customers. Additionally, by having a strong brand, you can also establish yourself as a valuable resource for pet owners and dog lovers, and differentiate yourself from competitors. Remember, creating a strong brand is an ongoing process, it's important to make it a priority in your business, and to constantly look for ways to improve and enhance your brand.

Building a Strong Community: Giving Back to Your Community

Giving back to your community is an important aspect of building a strong business and creating a positive impact. For dog boarding businesses, building a strong community can mean supporting local animal shelters and rescue groups, participating in community events, and promoting pet education and awareness. Here are some tips for building a strong community for your dog boarding business:

- Support local animal shelters and rescue groups: Support local animal shelters and rescue groups by donating a portion of your profits, volunteering your time, or hosting adoption events. This can help to raise awareness for animal welfare and promote the adoption of rescue dogs.
- Participate in community events: Participate in community events, such as pet fairs and parades, to promote your business and raise awareness for animal welfare.
- Promote pet education and awareness: Promote pet education and awareness by hosting seminars and workshops on topics such as dog training, behavior, and care. This can help to educate pet owners and raise awareness for responsible pet ownership.
- Partner with other pet-related businesses: Partner with other pet-related businesses, such as pet stores and veterinarians, to promote your services and raise awareness for animal welfare.
- Use social media to connect with your community: Use social media to connect with your community by

sharing information about upcoming events, animal welfare issues, and other pet-related news.

- Use your website to promote community involvement: Use your website to promote community involvement by sharing information about local animal shelters and rescue groups, as well as upcoming events and pet-related news.
- Provide a service to the community: Provide a service to the community by offering dog boarding for service and therapy animals, or offering training and rehabilitation services to dogs in need.

In addition to the tips mentioned above, there are a few more things to consider when building a strong community for your dog boarding business.

- Volunteer your time: Volunteer your time by participating in local animal welfare organizations and events, such as animal welfare campaigns, fostering animals in need, and participating in adoption events.
- Raise funds for animal welfare organizations: Raise funds for animal welfare organizations by organizing charity events, such as bake sales, car washes, and silent auctions.
- Use your platform to raise awareness: Use your platform to raise awareness about animal welfare issues and promote the adoption of rescue animals. Share information about animal welfare issues on social media, your website, and other marketing materials.
- Support animal welfare legislation: Support animal welfare legislation by contacting your local representatives and advocating for laws that protect animals.

- Support local shelters and rescues by hosting events: Support local shelters and rescues by hosting events such as open house days, adoption days, and other events at your business.
- Offer discounts to adopters: Offer discounts to customers who adopt a pet from a local animal shelter or rescue organization.

By volunteering your time, raising funds, using your platform to raise awareness, supporting animal welfare legislation, supporting local shelters and rescues by hosting events and offering discounts to adopters, you can build a strong community for your dog boarding business, make a positive impact on the lives of animals in your community, and promote responsible pet ownership. Remember, building a strong community is an ongoing process, it's important to make it a priority in your business, and to constantly look for ways to improve and enhance your community involvement. Additionally, by giving back to your community, you can also establish your business as a socially responsible and community-minded business, which will help to attract customers who are looking for a business that aligns with their values.

Building a Strong Referral Network: Creating a Support System

Creating a strong referral network is essential for any business, including a dog boarding business. A strong referral network can help to attract new customers, establish your business as a professional and credible provider of dog boarding services, and help to build trust with your customers. Here are some tips for building a strong referral network for your dog boarding business:

- Build relationships with other pet-related businesses: Build relationships with other pet-related businesses, such as veterinarians, pet stores, and dog trainers. This can help to create a support system of businesses that can refer customers to your dog boarding business.
- Build relationships with pet owners: Build relationships with pet owners by networking at community events, pet shows, and other pet-related events. This can help to create a support system of pet owners who can refer customers to your dog boarding business.
- Use social media to connect with pet owners: Use social media to connect with pet owners by sharing information about your dog boarding business, as well as pet-related news and events. This can help to create a support system of pet owners who can refer customers to your dog boarding business.
- Use your website to promote your referral network: Use your website to promote your referral network by sharing information about other pet-related businesses, as well as pet-related news and events. This can help to create a support system of businesses and pet owners

who can refer customers to your dog boarding business.

- Offer incentives for referrals: Offer incentives for referrals, such as discounts or referral bonuses, to encourage pet owners and other pet-related businesses to refer customers to your dog boarding business.
- Follow up with referrals: Follow up with referrals by sending thank-you notes or gifts to pet owners and other pet-related businesses who refer customers to your dog boarding business. This can help to create a support system of businesses and pet owners who can refer customers to your dog boarding business.

In addition to the tips mentioned above, there are a few more things to consider when building a strong referral network for your dog boarding business:

- Provide excellent customer service: Provide excellent customer service to all of your customers. This can help to create a positive reputation for your business, and increase the likelihood of customers referring their friends and family to your dog boarding business.
- Offer a referral program: Offer a referral program where customers can earn rewards for referring their friends and family to your dog boarding business. This can help to increase the number of referrals received and build a strong referral network.
- Ask for referrals: Ask for referrals from your current customers. Don't be afraid to ask your happy customers to refer their friends and family to your dog boarding business.

- Give back to your community: Give back to your community by supporting local animal shelters and rescue groups, participating in community events, and promoting pet education and awareness. This can help to create a positive reputation for your business, and increase the likelihood of customers referring their friends and family to your dog boarding business.
- Use customer testimonials: Use customer testimonials in your marketing materials. Share positive feedback from customers on your website, social media, and other marketing materials. This can help to create a positive reputation for your business, and increase the likelihood of customers referring their friends and family to your dog boarding business.

By providing excellent customer service, offering a referral program, asking for referrals, giving back to your community and using customer testimonials, you can build a strong referral network for your dog boarding business. Additionally, by providing excellent customer service, you can also establish your business as a reliable and trustworthy provider of dog boarding services, which will help to attract new customers and increase the likelihood of referrals. Remember, building a strong referral network is an ongoing process, it's important to make it a priority in your business, and to constantly look for ways to improve and enhance your referral network.

Building a Strong Online Presence: Optimizing Your Website for Search Engines

Having a strong online presence is essential for any business, including a dog boarding business. A strong online presence can help to attract new customers, establish your business as a professional and credible provider of dog boarding services, and help to build trust with your customers. One of the most important aspects of building a strong online presence is optimizing your website for search engines. Here are some tips for optimizing your website for search engines:

- Use relevant keywords: Use relevant keywords in your website's content, meta tags, and URLs. This can help search engines to understand the content of your website and improve your search engine rankings.
- Create high-quality content: Create high-quality content that is informative, engaging, and relevant. This can help to attract visitors to your website, and improve your search engine rankings.
- Use alt tags: Use alt tags to describe images on your website. This can help search engines to understand the content of your website and improve your search engine rankings.
- Use internal linking: Use internal linking to connect pages within your website. This can help search engines to understand the structure of your website, and improve your search engine rankings.
- Use external linking: Use external linking to connect your website to other relevant websites. This can help search engines to understand the relevance of your website, and improve your search engine rankings.

- Use social media: Use social media to connect with potential customers and promote your website. This can help to attract visitors to your website, and improve your search engine rankings.

In addition to the tips mentioned above, there are a few more things to consider when optimizing your website for search engines:

- Optimize your website for mobile devices: Optimize your website for mobile devices by making sure that it is responsive and easy to navigate on smaller screens. This can help to improve your search engine rankings, as more and more users are accessing the internet on their mobile devices.
- Use Schema markup: Use schema markup to add structured data to your website. This can help search engines to understand the content of your website and improve your search engine rankings.
- Use analytics: Use analytics to track the performance of your website. This can help you to identify areas of your website that need improvement, and make adjustments to improve your search engine rankings.
- Use a sitemap: Use a sitemap to organize the pages on your website. This can help search engines to understand the structure of your website, and improve your search engine rankings.
- Use a CDN: Use a Content Delivery Network (CDN) to speed up the loading time of your website. This can help to improve your search engine rankings, as well as the user experience for visitors to your website.

By optimizing your website for mobile devices, using schema markup, using analytics, using a sitemap and using a CDN, you can improve your website's search engine optimization and attract more visitors to your website. Additionally, by optimizing your website for mobile devices, you can also improve the user experience for visitors accessing your website on mobile devices, which can help to increase conversion rates and improve your online reputation. Remember, optimizing your website for search engines is an ongoing process, it's important to make it a priority in your business, and to constantly look for ways to improve and enhance your website's search engine optimization.

Building a Strong Email List: Keeping in Touch with Customers

Building a strong email list is an essential aspect of any business, including a dog boarding business. A strong email list can help to attract new customers, establish your business as a professional and credible provider of dog boarding services, and help to build trust with your customers. By keeping in touch with customers through email, you can also promote special deals and offers, and provide valuable content that will keep them engaged and interested in your business. Here are some tips for building a strong email list for your dog boarding business:

- Offer a sign-up incentive: Offer a sign-up incentive, such as a discount or free service, to encourage customers to join your email list.
- Make it easy to sign up: Make it easy for customers to sign up for your email list by placing sign-up forms on your website and social media pages, and in-store.
- Use a double opt-in process: Use a double opt-in process to confirm that customers want to receive emails from your business. This can help to ensure that your email list is made up of engaged and interested customers.
- Personalize your emails: Personalize your emails by addressing your customers by name, and including their interests and preferences in the content.
- Use a clear and consistent subject line: Use a clear and consistent subject line to make it easy for customers to understand the content of your emails.

- Provide valuable content: Provide valuable content in your emails, such as tips, information and news related to your business or the industry.
- Include calls to action: Include calls to action in your emails, such as special deals or offers, to encourage customers to take action.
- Use analytics: Use analytics to track the performance of your email campaigns and make adjustments to improve their effectiveness.

here are a few more things to consider when building a strong email list for your dog boarding business:

- Segment your list: Segment your email list based on factors such as customer preferences, past purchases or interests. This can help you to create more targeted and relevant email campaigns, which will be more likely to be opened and engaged with.
- Test your emails: Test different elements of your emails, such as subject lines, email content, and calls to action, to see which versions perform best. Use this information to improve your future email campaigns.
- Automate your emails: Automate your emails to save time and increase efficiency. For example, you can set up welcome emails for new subscribers, birthday or anniversary emails, and emails to promote special offers and deals.
- Use a professional email service provider: Use a professional email service provider such as Mailchimp, Constant Contact or AWeber to manage your email list and send your emails. These services will provide you with tools to create and track your email campaigns,

and will also help to ensure that your emails are delivered to your customers' inboxes.

- Keep your list clean: Regularly clean your email list by removing inactive or unengaged subscribers. This will help to ensure that your emails are being received by engaged and interested customers, which will improve the effectiveness of your email campaigns.
- Be compliant with laws: Be compliant with laws such as the CAN-SPAM act and GDPR, which regulate how businesses can use email for marketing purposes. This will help to ensure that your email campaigns are legal and will protect you from any potential legal issues.

By segmenting your list, testing your emails, automating your emails, using a professional email service provider, keeping your list clean and being compliant with laws, you can build a strong email list for your dog boarding business. Additionally, by building a strong email list, you can also establish yourself as a valuable resource for pet owners and dog lovers, and differentiate yourself from competitors. Remember, building a strong email list is an ongoing process, it's important to make it a priority in your business, and to constantly look for ways to improve and enhance your email list.

Building a Strong Customer Base: Building Loyalty and Trust

Building a strong customer base is crucial for the success of any business, including a dog boarding business. A strong customer base can provide a steady stream of revenue, help to promote your business through word-of-mouth advertising, and establish your business as a reputable and trustworthy provider of dog boarding services. Building loyalty and trust with your customers is essential for building a strong customer base. Here are some tips for building loyalty and trust with your customers:

- Provide excellent customer service: Provide excellent customer service by being responsive, friendly, and helpful. This can help to establish a positive reputation for your business and encourage customers to return.
- Be transparent: Be transparent in your business practices, such as pricing, policies and procedures. This can help to build trust with your customers, and make them more likely to return to your business.
- Communicate effectively: Communicate effectively with your customers by keeping them informed about their pet's stay and any changes or updates in your business. This can help to establish trust and build positive relationships with your customers.
- Show your expertise: Show your expertise in your field by providing valuable information, such as tips and advice, to your customers. This can help to establish your business as a credible and trustworthy resource for pet owners and dog lovers.

- Be consistent: Be consistent in the quality of your services, and the policies and procedures of your business. This can help to establish a positive reputation for your business and make customers more likely to return.
- Listen to your customers: Listen to your customers' feedback, complaints and concerns. This can help you to identify areas of your business that need improvement and make changes to improve customer satisfaction.
- Reward loyalty: Reward loyalty by offering special deals and discounts to regular customers. This can help to encourage customers to return to your business and build loyalty.

here are a few more things to consider when building a strong customer base for your dog boarding business:

- Get to know your customers: Get to know your customers by asking them about their pets, their likes and dislikes, and their needs. This can help you to personalize your services, and build stronger relationships with your customers.
- Follow up with your customers: Follow up with your customers after their pet's stay to ask for feedback and to check in on their pet. This can show that you care about the well-being of their pet and help to build loyalty.
- Build a sense of community: Build a sense of community by hosting events and activities, such as meet-ups or training classes, for your customers and their pets. This can help to foster a sense of belonging and build loyalty among your customers.

- Be available: Be available to your customers by providing a phone number and email that they can contact you on, and by responding to inquiries and messages in a timely manner. This can help to establish trust and make customers more likely to return to your business.
- Show appreciation: Show appreciation for your customers by sending thank-you notes, offering special deals or discounts, or hosting customer appreciation events. This can help to foster positive relationships and build loyalty.
- Seek customer feedback: Seek customer feedback by conducting surveys or focus groups, or by using online review sites. This can help you to identify areas of your business that need improvement, and make changes to improve customer satisfaction.
- Continuously improve: Continuously improve your services by staying informed about industry trends and advancements, and by incorporating new technologies and techniques to improve the overall customer experience.

By getting to know your customers, following up with them, building a sense of community, being available, showing appreciation, seeking customer feedback, and continuously improving, you can build a strong customer base for your dog boarding business. Additionally, by building a strong customer base, you can also establish your business as a reputable and trustworthy provider of dog boarding services, and differentiate yourself from competitors. Remember, building a strong customer base is an ongoing process, it's important to make it a priority in your business, and to constantly look for ways to improve and enhance your customer relationships.

Building a Strong Relationship with Suppliers: Finding the Right Vendors

Building a strong relationship with suppliers is essential for the success of any business, including a dog boarding business. A strong relationship with suppliers can help to ensure a steady supply of necessary goods and services, and can also help to establish a positive reputation for your business. Finding the right vendors is key to building a strong relationship with suppliers. Here are some tips for finding the right vendors for your dog boarding business:

- Research your options: Research your options by researching different suppliers and vendors, and by comparing prices, quality, and reputation. This can help you to identify the best suppliers for your business.
- Look for suppliers with a good reputation: Look for suppliers with a good reputation by reading customer reviews, asking for references and checking for any industry awards or certifications. This can help you to identify suppliers who are reliable and trustworthy.
- Consider location: Consider location by choosing suppliers that are located nearby. This can help to reduce shipping costs and transit times, and can also help to build a positive relationship with a local business.
- Look for suppliers that offer custom services: Look for suppliers that offer custom services, such as custom-made dog beds or specialized dog food. This can help you to offer unique and specialized services to your customers.

- Look for suppliers that offer bulk discounts: Look for suppliers that offer bulk discounts by buying in large quantities. This can help you to save money and reduce the need to constantly reorder supplies.
- Build a relationship: Build a relationship with your suppliers by regularly communicating with them, visiting their facilities, and keeping them informed about your business needs. This can help to establish trust and cooperation, and can also help you to identify any potential issues or opportunities.
- Negotiate: Negotiate prices, payment terms, and delivery schedules with your suppliers to get the best deals possible. This can help you to save money and make your business more competitive.
- Stay organized: Stay organized by keeping track of your orders, invoices, and delivery schedules, and by maintaining accurate records of your interactions with suppliers. This can help you to avoid any confusion or misunderstandings and to keep your business running smoothly.
- Create a backup plan: Create a backup plan by identifying alternative suppliers in case your primary supplier is unable to meet your needs. This can help you to minimize disruptions to your business and to ensure a steady supply of goods and services.
- Foster open communication: Foster open communication with your suppliers by providing them with clear, detailed, and accurate information about your needs, and by being responsive to their questions and concerns. This can help to build trust, cooperation and a better understanding of your needs
- Look for suppliers that offer additional services: Look for suppliers that offer additional services, such as

packaging, labeling, and branding. This can help you to minimize the need for additional vendors and to streamline your supply chain.

- Look for suppliers that are willing to work with you to resolve issues: Look for suppliers that are willing to work with you to resolve issues, such as damages or delays. This can help you to minimize disruptions to your business and to maintain positive relationships with your suppliers.

- Evaluate regularly: Evaluate your suppliers regularly by monitoring their performance and by assessing their pricing, quality and customer service. This can help you to identify areas of improvement and to make adjustments if needed.

By staying organized, creating a backup plan, fostering open communication, looking for suppliers that offer additional services, looking for suppliers that are willing to work with you to resolve issues and by evaluating regularly you can further strengthen your relationship with suppliers. By building strong relationships with suppliers, you can ensure a steady supply of goods and services, and can also establish your business as a reputable and trustworthy provider of dog boarding services. Remember, building strong relationship with suppliers is an ongoing process, it's important to make it a priority in your business, and to constantly look for ways to improve and enhance your supplier relationships.

Building a Strong Relationship with Local Veterinarians: Establishing a Medical Team

Building a strong relationship with local veterinarians is essential for the success of any dog boarding business. A strong relationship with local veterinarians can help to ensure the health and well-being of the dogs in your care, and can also help to establish a positive reputation for your business. Establishing a medical team is key to building a strong relationship with local veterinarians. Here are some tips for building a strong relationship with local veterinarians:

- Research your options: Research your options by researching different local veterinarians and their practices, and by comparing prices, quality, and reputation. This can help you to identify the best veterinarians for your business.
- Look for veterinarians with a good reputation: Look for veterinarians with a good reputation by reading customer reviews, asking for references and checking for any industry awards or certifications. This can help you to identify veterinarians who are reliable and trustworthy.
- Consider location: Consider location by choosing veterinarians that are located nearby. This can help to reduce transportation costs and times, and can also help to build a positive relationship with a local business.
- Look for veterinarians that offer emergency services: Look for veterinarians that offer emergency services, this can help you to ensure that the dogs in your care

receive prompt medical attention in case of an emergency.

- Schedule regular check-ups: Schedule regular check-ups for the dogs in your care with your chosen veterinarian, this can help you to ensure that the dogs are in good health and that any potential health issues are identified and addressed promptly.
- Build a relationship: Build a relationship with your chosen veterinarian by regularly communicating with them, visiting their facilities, and keeping them informed about the dogs in your care. This can help to establish trust and cooperation, and can also help you to identify any potential issues or opportunities.
- Seek their advice: Seek your veterinarian's advice when it comes to nutrition, behavior and training of dogs, this can help you to provide the best care possible and to keep your customers happy.
- Keep accurate medical records: Keep accurate medical records of the dogs in your care, including their vaccinations, medications and any other relevant information. This can help you to provide the best care possible, and to ensure that the dogs are healthy and safe while they are in your care.
- Communicate with the veterinarian: Communicate with the veterinarian regarding any concerns or observations you have about the dogs in your care. This can help you to identify any potential health issues and to ensure that the dogs receive prompt medical attention.
- Follow the veterinarian's instructions: Follow the veterinarian's instructions regarding the care and treatment of the dogs in your care. This can help you to ensure that the dogs receive the best care possible and that any health issues are addressed in a timely manner.

- Build a medical emergency plan: Build a medical emergency plan in case of an emergency, this can help you to ensure that the dogs in your care receive prompt medical attention.
- Build a relationship with other local pet service providers: Build a relationship with other local pet service providers, such as local groomers, trainers, and pet supply stores. This can help you to provide a complete range of services to your customers and to build a positive reputation in the community.
- Stay informed: Stay informed about the latest developments in veterinary medicine, by attending seminars, workshops, and by reading relevant publications. This can help you to provide the best care possible and to stay current with industry trends.

By keeping accurate medical records, communicating with the veterinarian, following the veterinarian's instructions, building a medical emergency plan, building a relationship with other local pet service providers, staying informed and by providing the best care possible, you can build a strong relationship with local veterinarians. Additionally, by building a strong relationship with local veterinarians, you can also establish your business as a reputable and trustworthy provider of dog boarding services, and differentiate yourself from competitors. Remember, building a strong relationship with local veterinarians is an ongoing process, it's important to make it a priority in your business, and to constantly look for ways to improve and enhance your relationship with local veterinarians.

Building a Strong Relationship with Pet Stores and Pet Supply Companies: Building Partnerships

Building a strong relationship with pet stores and pet supply companies is essential for the success of any dog boarding business. A strong relationship with pet stores and pet supply companies can help to ensure the health and well-being of the dogs in your care, and can also help to establish a positive reputation for your business. Building partnerships with pet stores and pet supply companies is key to building a strong relationship. Here are some tips for building a strong relationship with pet stores and pet supply companies:

- Research your options: Research your options by researching different pet stores and pet supply companies, and by comparing prices, quality, and reputation. This can help you to identify the best pet stores and pet supply companies for your business.
- Look for pet stores and pet supply companies with a good reputation: Look for pet stores and pet supply companies with a good reputation by reading customer reviews, asking for references and checking for any industry awards or certifications. This can help you to identify pet stores and pet supply companies who are reliable and trustworthy.
- Consider location: Consider location by choosing pet stores and pet supply companies that are located nearby. This can help to reduce transportation costs and times, and can also help to build a positive relationship with a local business.
- Look for pet stores and pet supply companies that offer a wide range of products: Look for pet stores and pet

supply companies that offer a wide range of products, this can help you to provide the best care possible for the dogs in your care.

- Schedule regular deliveries: Schedule regular deliveries with your chosen pet stores and pet supply companies, this can help you to ensure that you have a steady supply of necessary products.
- Build a relationship: Build a relationship with your chosen pet stores and pet supply companies by regularly communicating with them, visiting their facilities, and keeping them informed about the dogs in your care. This can help to establish trust and cooperation, and can also help you to identify any potential issues or opportunities.
- Seek their advice: Seek the advice of pet stores and pet supply companies when it comes to the best products for the dogs in your care, this can help you to provide the best care possible and to keep your customers happy.

By researching your options, looking for pet stores and pet supply companies with a good reputation, considering location, looking for pet stores and pet supply companies that offer a wide range of products, scheduling regular deliveries, building a relationship with your chosen pet stores and pet supply companies, seeking their advice and by keeping them informed about the dogs in your care, you can build a strong relationship with pet stores and pet supply companies. Additionally, by building a strong relationship with pet stores and pet supply companies, you can also establish your business as a reputable and trustworthy provider of dog boarding services, and differentiate yourself from competitors. Remember, building a strong relationship with pet stores and pet supply companies is an ongoing process, it's important to make it a priority in your business, and to constantly look for ways to improve and enhance your relationship with pet stores and pet supply companies.

Building a Strong Relationship with Pet Training and Behavior Specialists: Providing Additional Services

Building a strong relationship with pet training and behavior specialists is essential for the success of any dog boarding business. A strong relationship with pet training and behavior specialists can help to ensure the health and well-being of the dogs in your care, and can also help to establish a positive reputation for your business. Additionally, by providing additional services such as training and behavior modification, you can differentiate your business from competitors and attract new customers. Here are some tips for building a strong relationship with pet training and behavior specialists:

- Research your options: Research your options by researching different pet training and behavior specialists, and by comparing their qualifications, experience and reputation. This can help you to identify the best pet training and behavior specialists for your business.
- Look for pet training and behavior specialists with a good reputation: Look for pet training and behavior specialists with a good reputation by reading customer reviews, asking for references and checking for any industry awards or certifications. This can help you to identify pet training and behavior specialists who are reliable and trustworthy.
- Consider location: Consider location by choosing pet training and behavior specialists that are located nearby. This can help to reduce transportation costs

and times, and can also help to build a positive relationship with a local business.

- Look for pet training and behavior specialists that offer a wide range of services: Look for pet training and behavior specialists that offer a wide range of services, such as basic obedience training, behavior modification and socialization. This can help you to provide the best care possible for the dogs in your care.

- Schedule regular check-ins: Schedule regular check-ins with your chosen pet training and behavior specialists, this can help you to ensure that the dogs in your care receive the best training and behavior modification.

- Build a relationship: Build a relationship with your chosen pet training and behavior specialists by regularly communicating with them, visiting their facilities, and keeping them informed about the dogs in your care. This can help to establish trust and cooperation, and can also help you to identify any potential issues or opportunities.

- Seek their advice: Seek the advice of pet training and behavior specialists when it comes to the best training and behavior modification for the dogs in your care, this can help you to provide the best care possible and to keep your customers happy.

- Offer training and behavior modification as additional services: Offer training and behavior modification as additional services to your customers, this can help you to attract new customers and to differentiate your business from competitors.

when it comes to building a strong relationship with pet training and behavior specialists, it's important to not only focus on the qualifications, experience and reputation of the specialists, but also on how well they align with the goals and values of your business. It's important to look for pet training and behavior specialists who share a similar philosophy on training and behavior modification and who use methods that are in line with your own. Additionally, it's important to not only schedule regular check-ins with your chosen pet training and behavior specialists, but also to actively involve them in the training and behavior modification of the dogs in your care. This can include inviting them to observe the dogs in your care, and seeking their input and feedback on the progress of the dogs.

When it comes to offering additional services such as training and behavior modification, it's important to not only promote these services to your customers, but also to ensure that you have the necessary resources and expertise to provide these services effectively. This may include investing in additional training for yourself and your staff, as well as investing in equipment and resources such as training aids and behavior modification tools.

Another important aspect of building a strong relationship with pet training and behavior specialists is maintaining open and clear communication with them. This includes regularly updating them on the progress of the dogs in your care and seeking their input and feedback on any issues or concerns that arise. It's also important to be transparent with your customers about the involvement of pet training and behavior specialists in the care of their dogs, and to provide clear and detailed information about the services that you offer.

In summary, when it comes to building a strong relationship with pet training and behavior specialists, it's important to research your options, look for specialists with a good reputation, consider location, look for specialists that offer a wide range of services, schedule regular check-ins, build a relationship with your chosen specialists, seek their advice, offer training and behavior modification as additional services and maintain open and clear communication with them. Additionally, investing in resources and expertise, and being transparent with your customers about the involvement of pet training and behavior specialists in the care of their dogs is also important.

Building a Strong Relationship with Pet Rescue and Adoption Organizations: Supporting the Community

Building a strong relationship with pet rescue and adoption organizations is an important aspect of running a successful dog boarding business. Not only does it help to support the community, but it also helps to promote responsible pet ownership and can lead to new business opportunities. Pet rescue and adoption organizations are often in need of temporary foster homes and boarding facilities for animals in their care, and by establishing a positive relationship with these organizations, you can offer your services to help. Here are some tips for building a strong relationship with pet rescue and adoption organizations:

- Research your options: Research your options by researching different pet rescue and adoption organizations, and by comparing their missions, values, and the services they provide. This can help you to identify the best pet rescue and adoption organizations to partner with.
- Look for organizations with a good reputation: Look for organizations with a good reputation by reading customer reviews, asking for references, and checking for any industry awards or certifications. This can help you to identify organizations that are reliable and trustworthy.
- Consider location: Consider location by choosing organizations that are located nearby. This can help to reduce transportation costs and times, and can also

help to build a positive relationship with a local organization.

- Look for organizations that align with your values and mission: Look for organizations that align with your values and mission. For example, if you have a focus on rescuing and rehoming specific breeds, look for organizations that have the same focus.
- Schedule regular check-ins: Schedule regular check-ins with your chosen organizations, this can help you to stay informed about the animals in their care, and to identify any potential opportunities for collaboration.
- Build a relationship: Build a relationship with your chosen organizations by regularly communicating with them, visiting their facilities, and keeping them informed about the services you offer. This can help to establish trust and cooperation, and can also help you to identify any potential issues or opportunities.
- Seek their advice: Seek the advice of organizations when it comes to the best care and training for the animals in their care, this can help you to provide the best care possible and to keep your customers happy.
- Offer fostering and boarding as additional services: Offer fostering and boarding as additional services to your customers, this can help you to attract new customers, and to differentiate your business from competitors.
- Participate in events and fundraising: Participate in events and fundraising organized by the organizations, this can help to promote your business, and also help to support the community.

By researching your options, looking for organizations with a good reputation, considering location, looking for organizations that align with your values and mission, scheduling regular check-ins, building a relationship with your chosen organizations, seeking their advice, offering fostering and boarding as additional services, and participating in events and fundraising, you can build a strong relationship with pet rescue and adoption organizations. Additionally, by building a strong relationship with pet rescue and adoption organizations and by offering additional services such as fostering and boarding, you can establish your business as a reputable and trustworthy provider of dog boarding services, and differentiate yourself from competitors. Remember, building a strong relationship with pet rescue and adoption organizations is an ongoing process, it's important to make it a priority in your business, and to constantly look for ways to improve and enhance your relationship with pet rescue and adoption organizations. By supporting the community and promoting responsible pet ownership, you can be a valuable asset to the pet rescue and adoption organizations and the community.

Building a Strong Relationship with Pet Groomers: Providing Additional Services

Building a strong relationship with pet groomers is an important aspect of running a successful dog boarding business. Not only does it help to provide additional services to your customers, but it also helps to ensure that the dogs in your care are well-groomed and presentable. Pet groomers are experts in maintaining the hygiene and appearance of dogs, and by establishing a positive relationship with them, you can offer your services to help. Here are some tips for building a strong relationship with pet groomers:

- Research your options: Research your options by researching different pet groomers, and by comparing their qualifications, experience, and reputation. This can help you to identify the best pet groomers to partner with.
- Look for groomers with a good reputation: Look for groomers with a good reputation by reading customer reviews, asking for references, and checking for any industry awards or certifications. This can help you to identify groomers that are reliable and trustworthy.
- Consider location: Consider location by choosing groomers that are located nearby. This can help to reduce transportation costs and times, and can also help to build a positive relationship with a local groomer.
- Look for groomers that align with your values and mission: Look for groomers that align with your values and mission. For example, if you have a focus on

providing organic and natural grooming services, look for groomers that have the same focus.

- Schedule regular check-ins: Schedule regular check-ins with your chosen groomers, this can help you to stay informed about their services, and to identify any potential opportunities for collaboration.
- Build a relationship: Build a relationship with your chosen groomers by regularly communicating with them, visiting their facilities, and keeping them informed about the services you offer. This can help to establish trust and cooperation, and can also help you to identify any potential issues or opportunities.
- Seek their advice: Seek the advice of groomers when it comes to the best grooming practices and products for the dogs in your care, this can help you to provide the best care possible and to keep your customers happy.
- Offer grooming as an additional service: Offer grooming as an additional service to your customers, this can help you to attract new customers, and to differentiate your business from competitors.
- Cross-promote your services: Cross-promote your services with the groomers, this can help to promote your business, and also help to increase the visibility of the groomer's business.
- Utilize their services: Utilize the services of pet groomers to keep the dogs in your care well-groomed and presentable. This can help to attract new customers and to build a strong reputation for your business.
- Offer discounts: Offer discounts to customers who use the services of the groomers you partner with. This can help to encourage customers to use your services and the services of the groomers you partner with.

- Collaborate on events: Collaborate with pet groomers on events such as pet shows, adoption events, and other pet-related events. This can help to promote your business and the business of the groomers you partner with.
- Share your expertise: Share your expertise with pet groomers. For example, if you have experience in training dogs, you can offer training classes or workshops to groomers. This can help to establish yourself as an expert in the field and can also help to build a strong relationship with pet groomers.
- Be open to feedback: Be open to feedback from pet groomers. Listen to their suggestions, and be willing to make changes to improve your services. This can help to establish trust and cooperation, and can also help you to identify any potential issues or opportunities.
- Be professional: Be professional and respectful when interacting with pet groomers. This can help to establish trust and cooperation, and can also help to build a strong reputation for your business.
- Continuously improve: Continuously improve your services and your relationship with pet groomers. This can help to attract new customers and to build a strong reputation for your business.

In conclusion, building a strong relationship with pet groomers is an important aspect of running a successful dog boarding business. By researching your options, looking for groomers with a good reputation, considering location, looking for groomers that align with your values and mission, scheduling regular check-ins, building a relationship with your chosen groomers, seeking their advice, offering grooming as an additional service, cross-promoting your services, utilizing their services, offering discounts, collaborating on events, sharing your expertise, being open to feedback, being professional, and continuously improving, you can establish a positive and productive partnership with pet groomers. Additionally, by offering additional services such as grooming, you can attract new customers and differentiate your business from competitors. Remember, building a strong relationship with pet groomers is an ongoing process, it's important to make it a priority in your business and to constantly look for ways to improve and enhance your relationship with pet groomers.

Building a Strong Relationship with Pet Photographers: Providing Additional Services

Building a strong relationship with pet photographers is an important aspect of running a successful dog boarding business. Not only does it help to provide additional services to your customers, but it also helps to showcase the dogs in your care in the best light possible. Pet photographers are experts in capturing the beauty and personality of dogs, and by establishing a positive relationship with them, you can offer your services to help. Here are some tips for building a strong relationship with pet photographers:

- Research your options: Research your options by researching different pet photographers, and by comparing their qualifications, experience, and reputation. This can help you to identify the best pet photographers to partner with.
- Look for photographers with a good reputation: Look for photographers with a good reputation by reading customer reviews, asking for references, and checking for any industry awards or certifications. This can help you to identify photographers that are reliable and trustworthy.
- Consider location: Consider location by choosing photographers that are located nearby. This can help to reduce transportation costs and times, and can also help to build a positive relationship with a local photographer.
- Look for photographers that align with your values and mission: Look for photographers that align with your values and mission. For example, if you have a focus on

providing organic and natural boarding services, look for photographers that have the same focus.

- Schedule regular check-ins: Schedule regular check-ins with your chosen photographers, this can help you to stay informed about their services, and to identify any potential opportunities for collaboration.
- Build a relationship: Build a relationship with your chosen photographers by regularly communicating with them, visiting their facilities, and keeping them informed about the services you offer. This can help to establish trust and cooperation, and can also help you to identify any potential issues or opportunities.
- Seek their advice: Seek the advice of photographers when it comes to the best ways to showcase the dogs in your care, this can help you to provide the best care possible and to keep your customers happy.
- Offer photography as an additional service: Offer photography as an additional service to your customers, this can help you to attract new customers, and to differentiate your business from competitors.
- Cross-promote your services: Cross-promote your services with the photographers, this can help to promote your business, and also help to increase the visibility of the photographer's business.

By researching your options, looking for photographers with a good reputation, considering location, looking for photographers that align with your values and mission, scheduling regular check-ins, building a relationship with your chosen photographers, seeking their advice, offering photography as an additional service, and cross-promote your services, you can build a strong relationship with pet photographers. Additionally, by building a strong relationship with pet photographers and by offering additional services such as photography, you can establish your business as a reputable and trustworthy provider of dog boarding services, and differentiate yourself from competitors. Remember, building a strong relationship with pet photographers is an ongoing process, it's important to make it a priority in your business, and to constantly look for ways to improve and enhance your relationship with pet photographers. By providing additional services and working with reputable pet photographers, you can showcase the dogs in your care in the best light possible, which can help to attract new customers and to build a strong reputation for your business.

Building a Strong Relationship with Pet Transportation Services: Providing Additional Services

Building a strong relationship with pet transportation services is an important aspect of running a successful dog boarding business. Not only does it help to provide additional services to your customers, but it also helps to ensure that the dogs in your care are safely and comfortably transported to and from your facility. Pet transportation services are experts in safely transporting pets, and by establishing a positive relationship with them, you can offer your services to help. Here are some tips for building a strong relationship with pet transportation services:

- Research your options: Research your options by researching different pet transportation services, and by comparing their qualifications, experience, and reputation. This can help you to identify the best pet transportation services to partner with.
- Look for services with a good reputation: Look for services with a good reputation by reading customer reviews, asking for references, and checking for any industry awards or certifications. This can help you to identify transportation services that are reliable and trustworthy.
- Consider location: Consider location by choosing transportation services that are located nearby. This can help to reduce transportation costs and times, and can also help to build a positive relationship with a local service.

- Look for services that align with your values and mission: Look for services that align with your values and mission. For example, if you have a focus on providing organic and natural boarding services, look for transportation services that have the same focus.
- Schedule regular check-ins: Schedule regular check-ins with your chosen transportation services, this can help you to stay informed about their services, and to identify any potential opportunities for collaboration.
- Build a relationship: Build a relationship with your chosen transportation services by regularly communicating with them, visiting their facilities, and keeping them informed about the services you offer. This can help to establish trust and cooperation, and can also help you to identify any potential issues or opportunities.
- Seek their advice: Seek the advice of transportation services when it comes to the best ways to transport the dogs in your care, this can help you to provide the best care possible and to keep your customers happy.
- Offer transportation as an additional service: Offer transportation as an additional service to your customers, this can help you to attract new customers, and to differentiate your business from competitors.
- Cross-promote your services: Cross-promote your services with the transportation services, this can help to promote your business, and also help to increase the visibility of the transportation service's business.
- Ensure compliance: Make sure that the transportation service you choose is compliant with all the relevant laws and regulations, this can help you to avoid any legal issues and fines.

-Consider the type of transportation: Consider the type of transportation the service offers, for example, whether it's ground transportation or air transportation. This can help you to choose a service that can meet the specific needs of your customers.

- Collaborate on marketing efforts: Collaborating on marketing efforts with pet transportation services can help to increase awareness of your business, and can also help to attract new customers. This can include joint promotions, advertising, and social media campaigns.
- Offer a bundle package: Offer a bundle package that includes both dog boarding services and transportation services. This can help to simplify the process for customers, and can also help to increase revenue for your business.
- Establish a communication protocol: Establish a clear communication protocol with your pet transportation services, this can help to ensure that all parties are on the same page, and can also help to avoid any misunderstandings or confusion.
- Provide feedback: Provide feedback to your transportation services, this can help to improve their services, and can also help to ensure that they are meeting the needs of your customers.
- Continuously evaluate the partnership: Continuously evaluate the partnership with your transportation services, this can help to ensure that it is still meeting your business's needs, and can also help to identify any areas for improvement.
- Seek out transportation services that specialize in dog transportation: Seek out transportation services that

specialize in dog transportation, this can help to ensure that the dogs in your care are transported in a safe and comfortable manner.

- Prioritize safety: Prioritize safety when it comes to transportation, this can help to ensure that the dogs in your care are transported in a safe and secure manner, and can also help to reduce the risk of accidents.
- Provide clear instructions: Provide clear instructions to your transportation services, this can help to ensure that all parties are on the same page, and can also help to avoid any misunderstandings or confusion.

By collaborating on marketing efforts, offering a bundle package, establishing a communication protocol, providing feedback, continuously evaluating the partnership, seeking out transportation services that specialize in dog transportation, prioritizing safety, and providing clear instructions, you can build a strong relationship with pet transportation services and provide additional services that meet the needs of your customers. Additionally, by building a strong relationship with pet transportation services, you can ensure that the dogs in your care are safely and comfortably transported, and that your customers are satisfied with the services you provide.

Building a Strong Relationship with Pet Insurance Companies: Providing Additional Services

Building a strong relationship with pet insurance companies is an important aspect of running a successful dog boarding business. Not only does it help to provide additional services to your customers, but it also helps to ensure that the dogs in your care are protected in the event of an emergency. Pet insurance companies are experts in providing coverage for pet-related expenses, and by establishing a positive relationship with them, you can offer your services to help. Here are some tips for building a strong relationship with pet insurance companies:

- Research your options: Research your options by researching different pet insurance companies, and by comparing their coverage, pricing, and reputation. This can help you to identify the best pet insurance companies to partner with.
- Look for companies with a good reputation: Look for companies with a good reputation by reading customer reviews, asking for references, and checking for any industry awards or certifications. This can help you to identify insurance companies that are reliable and trustworthy.
- Consider the coverage offered: Consider the coverage offered by the insurance companies, this can help you to choose a company that can meet the specific needs of your customers.
- Look for companies that align with your values and mission: Look for companies that align with your values and mission. For example, if you have a focus on

providing organic and natural boarding services, look for insurance companies that have the same focus.

- Schedule regular check-ins: Schedule regular check-ins with your chosen insurance companies, this can help you to stay informed about their services, and to identify any potential opportunities for collaboration.
- Build a relationship: Build a relationship with your chosen insurance companies by regularly communicating with them, visiting their facilities, and keeping them informed about the services you offer. This can help to establish trust and cooperation, and can also help you to identify any potential issues or opportunities.
- Seek their advice: Seek the advice of insurance companies when it comes to the best ways to protect the dogs in your care, this can help you to provide the best care possible and to keep your customers happy.
- Offer insurance as an additional service: Offer insurance as an additional service to your customers, this can help you to attract new customers, and to differentiate your business from competitors.
- Cross-promote your services: Cross-promote your services with the insurance companies, this can help to promote your business, and also help to increase the visibility of the insurance company's business.
- Ensure compliance: Make sure that the insurance company you choose is compliant with all the relevant laws and regulations, this can help you to avoid any legal issues and fines.

- Offer discounts for customers who purchase insurance: Offer discounts for customers who purchase insurance through your business, this can help to incentivize customers to purchase insurance, and can also help to increase revenue for your business.
- Keep updated with the latest policies: Keep updated with the latest policies of the insurance companies you partner with, this can help you to ensure that you are providing accurate information to your customers, and can also help you to identify any changes that may affect your business.
- Provide customer service: Provide customer service to customers who purchase insurance through your business, this can help to ensure that they are satisfied with their purchase, and can also help to identify any potential issues or concerns.
- Educate your customers: Educate your customers about the benefits of pet insurance, this can help to increase awareness and understanding of the product, and can also help to increase sales.
- Build trust and credibility: Build trust and credibility by providing accurate and reliable information about pet insurance, this can help to establish your business as a reputable and trustworthy provider of dog boarding services and insurance.
- Maintain transparency: Maintain transparency by providing your customers with clear and detailed information about the insurance policies and coverage offered, this can help to establish trust and credibility with your customers.
- Provide additional resources: Provide additional resources such as brochures, flyers, and website links that provide information about pet insurance, this can

help to increase awareness and understanding of the product.

By offering discounts for customers who purchase insurance, keeping updated with the latest policies, providing customer service, educating your customers, building trust and credibility, maintaining transparency, and providing additional resources, you can strengthen your relationship with pet insurance companies and help to increase sales of insurance. Additionally, by providing customer service and education, you can ensure that your customers are satisfied with their purchase and understand the benefits of pet insurance. By building trust and credibility, you can establish your business as a reputable and trustworthy provider of dog boarding services and insurance.

Conclusion: Taking Your Dog Boarding Business to the Next Level

Starting a dog boarding business can be a rewarding and fulfilling endeavor, but it also requires a significant investment of time, money, and energy. By following the step-by-step guide outlined in this book, you can set your business up for success, and take it to the next level.

When it comes to taking your dog boarding business to the next level, there are a few key areas to focus on:

- Continuously assessing the market: Continuously assessing the market and identifying your target audience will help you to stay ahead of trends, and to adapt your business to meet the changing needs of your customers.
- Developing a strong business plan: Developing a strong business plan, setting goals and objectives, and regularly reviewing and updating your plan can help you to stay on track and to achieve your business goals.
- Finding the right location: Choosing the right property, and creating a safe and comfortable space for your four-legged guests can help you to attract customers and to establish your business as a reputable and trustworthy provider of dog boarding services.
- Obtaining licenses and permits: Complying with local regulations, obtaining licenses and permits, and staying up-to-date with the latest laws and regulations can help you to avoid any legal issues and fines, and to establish your business as a reputable and trustworthy provider of dog boarding services.

- Creating a marketing plan: Creating a marketing plan, advertising and promoting your business, and building a strong online presence can help you to attract new customers, and to establish your business as a reputable and trustworthy provider of dog boarding services.
- Hiring staff: Finding the right team, and providing training and education can help you to provide the best care possible, and to keep your customers happy.
- Setting rates and policies: Setting rates and policies, and establishing your business structure can help you to stay competitive and to attract new customers.
- Providing quality care: Meeting the needs of your four-legged guests, and providing a home-like experience can help you to attract new customers and to build repeat business.
- Keeping accurate records: Managing your finances, and keeping accurate records can help you to stay on top of your expenses, and to make informed business decisions.
- Building relationships: Networking with other pet professionals, building relationships with local veterinarians, pet stores, and pet supply companies, and giving back to your community can help you to establish your business as a reputable and trustworthy provider of dog boarding services, and to build a strong reputation in the community.
- Keeping up with industry trends: Staying current in the dog boarding business, and keeping up with industry trends can help you to stay ahead of the competition and to attract new customers.
- Building a strong reputation: Managing your online presence, building a strong reputation, and building a

strong community can help you to attract new customers, and to establish your business as a reputable and trustworthy provider of dog boarding services.

- Offering additional services: Expanding your business by offering additional services such as grooming, photography, transportation, and training, can help you to attract new customers, and to increase revenue.
- Building a strong website: Creating an online presence, building a strong website, and utilizing social media can help you to attract new customers, and to establish your business as a reputable and trustworthy provider of dog boarding services.
- Building a strong brand: Developing your business identity, building a strong brand, and creating a strong community can help you to attract new customers, and to establish your business as a reputable and trustworthy provider of dog boarding services.
- Building repeat business: Retaining customers by providing quality care, building strong relationships, and offering additional services can help you to increase revenue and establish a loyal customer base.
- Handling difficult situations: Dealing with complaints and issues in a professional and timely manner can help you to maintain a positive reputation and to build trust with your customers.
- Insurance and liability: Protecting your business by obtaining the necessary insurance and complying with liability laws can help you to avoid potential legal issues and to provide peace of mind for your customers.
- Building a strong referral network: Creating a support system by building relationships with other pet professionals and fostering a strong community can

help you to attract new customers and to establish your business as a reputable and trustworthy provider of dog boarding services.

- Building a strong online presence: Optimizing your website for search engines and building a strong email list can help you to attract new customers and to establish your business as a reputable and trustworthy provider of dog boarding services.
- Building a strong customer base: Building loyalty and trust by providing quality care, building strong relationships, and offering additional services can help you to attract new customers and to establish a loyal customer base.
- Building a strong relationship with suppliers: Finding the right vendors, building trust, and maintaining transparency can help you to provide the best products and services for your customers.
- Building a strong relationship with local veterinarians: Establishing a medical team, building trust, and maintaining transparency can help you to provide the best care for your four-legged guests and to establish your business as a reputable and trustworthy provider of dog boarding services.
- Building a strong relationship with pet stores and pet supply companies: Building partnerships, building trust, and maintaining transparency can help you to provide the best products and services for your customers.
- Building a strong relationship with pet training and behavior specialists: Providing additional services, building trust, and maintaining transparency can help you to provide the best care for your four-legged guests and to establish your business as a reputable and trustworthy provider of dog boarding services.

- Building a strong relationship with pet rescue and adoption organizations: Supporting the community, building trust, and maintaining transparency can help you to establish your business as a reputable and trustworthy provider of dog boarding services and to make a positive impact on the community.

In conclusion, starting a dog boarding business is a challenging but rewarding endeavor. By following the steps outlined in this guide, and focusing on key areas such as market assessment, business planning, location selection, licensing and permits, marketing, staffing, quality care, record keeping, building relationships, industry trends, reputation management, additional services, website development, and insurance and liability, you can set your business up for success and take it to the next level. Remember to always be open to learning and adapting, as the dog boarding industry is constantly evolving and it's important to stay up to date with the latest trends and developments.

"Starting a dog boarding business is a rewarding and fulfilling journey. We hope that this guide has provided you with the information, tips, and resources you need to start and grow your business. Remember to focus on providing quality care, building strong relationships, and staying up-to-date with industry trends. With hard work, dedication, and a passion for dogs, you can build a successful and thriving business. We wish you all the best on your journey and look forward to hearing about your success. Remember, every dog deserves a loving and comfortable home away from home, and you have the power to make that happen. Good luck!"